CHASING COYOTES
Accounts of Urban Crises

CHASING COYOTES

Accounts of Urban Crises

Debora Martin

ATLAS PUBLISHING
SOLANA BEACH, CALIFORNIA

CHASING COYOTES: *Accounts of Urban Crises*

Published by 🔺 Atlas Publishing

Permission requests and other queries should be addressed to the publisher:

Managing Editor
Atlas Publishing
PO Box 1730
Solana Beach CA 92075
permissions@atlaspublishing.biz
www.atlaspublishing.biz

Library of Congress Control Number: 2016956027
ISBN-13: 978-1-945033-24-7

1 3 5 7 9 8 6 4 2

First edition. Published and printed in the United States of America.

This book is dedicated to the thousands of pets throughout North America who have lost their lives to coyotes, and to their owners, who have experienced and continue to feel the painful loss of their beloved pets.

CONTENTS

1

Introduction

Let me begin by noting that I am not a wildlife biologist. In fact, my degrees and certifications are in fields entirely unrelated to wildlife biology. The information I am about to share comes from my own experiences with urban coyotes, hundreds of hours spent researching coyotes throughout North America, and information to which I have been privy as the director of Coyotes in Orange County, CA (abbreviated Coyotes OC for the remainder of this book). This book's purpose is fourfold: (1) to document the plight of urban coyotes in North America, (2) to reduce the amount of misinformation presently circulating about urban coyotes, (3) to remove or reduce any fear the reader may have of coyotes, and (4) to encourage readers to haze coyotes every time they see them (hazing is described in greater detail in the chapters that follow).

Coyotes are dynamic creatures, and their innate ability to effectively adapt to any environment is what makes them such amazing creatures. One cannot study coyotes without developing an admiration for them and their remarkable skills. Because coyotes are continually learning and adapting to environments, they are also constantly changing their behavior, which makes some prior information about coyotes obsolete. The goal of animal rights groups is to persuade people to coexist with coyotes, and they accomplish this goal by saying anything that may sway your opinion toward their point of view. Unfortunately, this results in the intentional and unintentional spreading of untruths and the suppression of information not supporting their views. This misinformation creates confusion and discourages people from taking the proper and necessary steps to effectively protect themselves, their families, and their pets from coyotes. My hope is to provide enough information to help readers quickly and effectively handle any situation that may arise involving coyotes.

Keeping people and their pets safe has always been my first priority. Sometimes keeping people and pets safe, however, makes coexistence with coyotes more challenging. Lethal management is normally used only as a last resort after coyotes have become fearless of humans (habituated). However, we must be careful to not exclude lethal management completely, as doing so limits the options for keeping people safe.

2

THE BEGINNING

There was a time, which now seems long ago, when residents of California communities entertained family and friends by barbecuing, swimming, and playing croquet, shuffleboard, or horseshoes in their backyards without being concerned about four-legged trespassers with teeth. Cats roamed in front and back yards freely and safely. Dogs enjoyed the peaceful serenity of their own backyard playgrounds day and night.

When I was growing up in Orange County, a dog would occasionally get loose; the gate was not closed securely, or the dog managed to jump over a wall or fence. My brothers and I would spend considerable time looking for our dog when this happened. We often found our dog either down the street at a neighbor's house or in the nearby field chasing mice, gophers, or rabbits. And on those rare occasions when we could not find our dog, we knew we could look for

him at the local animal shelter. The few times we did
so, we found our dog at the shelter in a kennel, joyfully
wagging his tail and very happy to see us.

The era of the 1960s was a vastly different time
from today. As children, we were adventurous and
found many ways to keep ourselves entertained. We
took a minibike or a motorcycle to local fields and rode
all day. We traveled two miles down Warner Avenue
to the Santa Ana River, rented horses, and rode them
up and down the sandy riverbed banks. Plenty of
wildlife along the Santa Ana River could always be
seen and enjoyed: raccoons, birds of all types, skunks,
weasels, squirrels, gophers, lizards, rats, mice, and rabbits. We rode our bicycles to the lakes at Mile Square
Regional Park and spent the day there mastering our
stone-skipping techniques. We went to the local farm-
ers' fields along Warner Avenue, Slater Avenue, and
Brookhurst Street after harvest and picked fresh corn
and asparagus. We even created our own adventures
such as exploring the channels and storm drains in
our neighborhood. We discovered just how easy it was
to enter the storm drains and channels. This resulted
in quite a few adventures for us over the course of several years. However, during all of our activities and
adventures in the 1960s, we never once saw a coyote
or a fox.

One by one, the horse stables located along the Santa Ana River disappeared. Open fields were developed into homes, condominiums, apartment complexes, schools, gas stations, strip malls, commercial buildings, and a drive-in movie theater. Even Mile Square Regional Park was further developed, with a recreational facility added for residents to enjoy racquetball, basketball, baseball, and tennis. Four decades passed, yet we never heard or saw coyotes or foxes in our city. With all the development and growth our city experienced over four decades, it's surprising that we never saw the coyotes and foxes that lived nearby.

How and when did all this change? Urban coyote encounters have become more frequent, and with increased habituation of coyotes, more dangerous. Of even greater concern, this problem that I first observed in Southern California has become a crisis in urban areas throughout the United States, Canada, and Central America.

Some people say the coyote population has been growing for many years, maybe even decades. Those same people say they are not surprised by the coyote overpopulation problem that we are seeing today. Others never knew that coyotes and foxes were living in their cities. The story told by community elders is that the coyotes and foxes that had inhabited our local parks and open land areas were content to stay in those areas as long as the ecosystem could support them. Because the ecosystem was sufficient to meet their needs, coyotes and foxes remained invisible for many years, only coming out during late evening or very early morning hours. When people saw a coyote or a fox, they probably mistook it for a dog.

Coyotes and foxes remained in our parks and open areas until they dared to venture outside of those areas. When coyotes discovered that humans were good providers of food sources—such as trash, fruit, livestock, and pets—they continued hunting and scavenging for food in the neighborhoods surrounding parks and open areas. Coyotes and foxes learned that they could travel freely and undetected throughout the city via storm drains, channels, and rivers, which became coyote superhighways.

Foxes coexisted with coyotes and learned to use the same travel corridors. Coyotes began to thrive, and their population grew even larger. In the city, virtually all the natural coyote predators were either gone or had never existed.

In 2010, we first began to hear of coyote problems in the residential areas surrounding Mile Square Regional Park.[1] Many strip malls had restaurants, and residents believed that open dumpsters were attracting coyotes to their neighborhoods. Heated complaints by residents were voiced at city council meetings, but nothing was ever done to address the problem. When I learned of the coyote problems faced by residents

around Mile Square Regional Park, I remember thinking how grateful I was that I lived miles from the park.
Little did I know what was about to happen in my own
neighborhood.

At the same time, my friend Judy Oswald and
I were dealing with stray cats in our neighborhood,
which was beginning to resemble a cat community
with all the stray and feral cats. On any given day,
one could stroll through my condominium complex
and see a dozen cats sleeping on the sidewalks and
in common areas. The stray cat problem resulted from
irresponsible pet owners (mostly renters) who aban-
doned and left their cats behind when they moved,
or refused to spay or neuter their cats. Our stray cat
problem grew so large that they were wandering into
residents' garages through open doors and giving
birth to litters of kittens.

That is exactly what happened to my neighbor,
Jerry Nuzzo. A pregnant six-month-old female cat
(still a baby herself) had wandered into his garage and
delivered four kittens. Jerry, who was in his seventies
at the time, was not even aware he had cats living in
his garage until one day he saw the kittens. Soon after,
Jerry suffered a stroke and was hospitalized. I fed the
family of cats for Jerry while he was in the hospital.
A month passed, and the mother cat and one of the
four kittens wandered off and left the remaining three

kittens in Jerry's garage. I still hoped that Jerry would return home again, even after I was told that he had been moved into a rehabilitation facility.

When we discovered that a second cat had wandered into another neighbor's garage and given birth to six kittens, both Judy and I agreed that something needed to be done about the stray cat problem in our neighborhood. Judy owned a live trap, and we decided to trap the cats, one by one, and take them to a veterinarian to have them treated for worms and fleas, vaccinated, and fixed. None of these cats and kittens had names (at least none of which we were aware), so we named them. We quickly and easily trapped and treated the first two kittens: Little Girl and Big Boy. We still had two to catch, however: a kitten we called Orange and a cat we called Momma Kitty.

Orange was the last of the three kittens from Jerry's garage—a beautiful golden long-haired male cat. He was also the most skittish of the three kittens, which made him very difficult to catch. Momma Kitty had just given birth to a litter of six kittens; only two remained. A neighbor told us he had taken four of the kittens to the animal shelter. Momma Kitty was a very small cat and looked like the runt of a litter, but could she run! I cannot tell you how many times I chased Momma Kitty through the complex trying to catch her. We managed to capture Momma Kitty's remaining two kittens and sent them along with some money to a friend in Newport Beach to domesticate the feral kittens and find homes for them.

It took some time, but we eventually caught and treated Orange and Momma Kitty. When Jerry passed away, we needed to find homes for his three kittens, which were now 9 months old, and Momma Kitty, who was now more than a year old. All four cats were unfriendly and wanted nothing to do with people. They hissed at people and ran from them; they were strays and behaved like feral cats. Judy told me if we took these cats to the animal shelter, they would be put down because they were not adoptable. I knew she was right, so we continued looking for homes for the cats.

Soon after that, another feral female kitten wandered into our complex. We figured she was maybe 10 weeks old when we caught her, and we sent her to our friend in Newport Beach to be domesticated and adopted out. It was strange to find only one kitten and no mother cat or siblings. We trapped and treated a total of seven cats in 2010, and never saw stray kittens in our community again.

It was not until summer 2011 that coyotes found their way down the Fountain Valley and Talbert channels and into the southern part of Fountain Valley where my condominium complex was located. I remember awakening at 3:30 a.m. to a cat screaming, and a growling sound like I had never heard before. I was frozen with fear as I lay in my bed and prayed that the screaming and growling sounds were not those of one of my cats. I had two cats of my own, but had recently adopted Jerry's three cats, for a total of four males and one female. I was so terrified by the sounds I heard that morning that I could not even lift myself out of bed to investigate, and I never could get back to sleep that night.

The next morning, I counted cats before I went to work and only counted four—Big Boy was missing. I hoped that Big Boy was only hiding and would come home eventually, but he never did. It was a day or two later when I learned what had happened that morning. A 16-year-old boy's bedroom window overlooked the area where the attack occurred, and he saw the whole thing. A coyote had attacked a black cat, and even though the cat put up a good fight, he was no match for the coyote. All the coyote left of Big Boy was his intestines and one leg.

Mary Lundergan, a board member for our homeowners' association (HOA), told me the boy's story of the attack and what she had discovered afterward. I told Mary that I heard the attack and was afraid that it was Big Boy, because he had never returned home. Neither of us had experienced anything like this before, even though we had both lived here for more than 30 years. I advised Mary that we should put the information about the attack in the community news-letter, because residents needed be warned about the coyote. (Working in the insurance industry, I knew that warning residents of coyotes in the neighborhood via the newsletter would also release the association from potential liability in the event of future coyote attacks.) It was fortuitous that we put the information about the coyote attack in the newsletter, because this was only the first of many attacks.

At the same time, just a few miles away in the neighboring city of Huntington Beach, Carolyn Graf Matthews lost her cat, Mickey, to a coyote. In her own words:

> At 5:00 a.m., a coyote came down our street. I had an older female cat, Tilly, and then a younger fluff ball of a male cat, Mickey, who thought he was very tough. Mickey tried to protect his older companion, Tilly, and in doing so he lost his life.
>
> A neighbor was outside getting ready to leave for work. They are the ones who wit-nessed this and tried to help the cat. They were unable to help, but they let us know what had happened. I, too, was just about to leave for work when a neighbor knocked on my front door. Normally, I would have been outside on my driveway, but I was not because I had been in a car accident just the week before and was in a lot of pain.

Mickey was 12 years old. He was a Himalayan cat. He was a tolerant and gentle cat. He was also not very athletic and could not climb a fence. Both cats enjoyed laying on our patio or the front driveway and sitting in the sun. Mickey did not wander off; neither cat did. They came when called, like dogs, and slept inside every night. Mickey let kids do anything to him; my youngest dragged him around like a rag doll—he went limp and never scratched. When I rescued him from these encounters, he just purred away and held no grudges. He behaved more like a dog than like a cat.

The litter boxes were in the garage, and the main garage door was open only about five inches from the floor.

Mickey and Tilly probably had just gone out to use the litter boxes. It was 5:00 a.m. Tilly had gone to lie on the driveway and was soaking up the morning sun. Mickey, still in the garage, must have been keeping an eye on her. The coyote came down the street and Mickey saw Tilly was in trouble. Mickey ran out and came to defend his older companion. Tilly ran back into the garage for safety and witnessed Mickey being killed as he tried to defend her. Mickey was left on the sidewalk and the coyote ran off seeing the neighbors run toward him.

Tilly never was the same. She would not leave the darkest corner of the garage and would not eat. We relocated her, but each time she would return to the garage and hide. She continued to not eat and pulled out her fur.

I went around my neighborhood and found out that other neighbors had recently lost cats and dogs to coyotes as well. I found that most were like me, with no clue that coyotes were in the area and killing everyone's pets. Never had there been such a problem! I was surprised that people were not informing their neighbors.

I was mad, too! Had any of my neighbors gone door-to-door as we had, maybe my cat would still be alive. I called animal control, the police, and multiple agencies, and was pushed off like a nuisance. No one cared! No one was in charge of the problem! I was mad!

A couple weeks after Mickey died, I found out that I had a broken back and would need major surgery. Meanwhile, I had lost both my cats.

I had to wait several months for my back surgery, and was told that physical therapy would not be possible for the first 3 months following surgery, with more months of therapy after that. Having just lost both my cats and with time on my hands, I decided to put it to good use, and that is when I created the website Coyotes in Orange County, CA (Coyotes OC). I wanted people to have a place to find facts, to learn how to protect their pets, and to learn more about what was happening in their neighborhoods. I later found that the reports being taken about pets being killed were not even being logged, and those agencies that actually did log reports would not share that information. That is when I created the Coyote Tracking System, enabling people to log when and where attacks took place.

On November 14, 2011, Carolyn Graf Matthews launched Coyotes OC on Facebook.

When a coyote attacks and kills someone's pet, the pet is not the only victim. The pet owner is a victim as well, because of trauma resulting from the attack. In the coyote attack on Carolyn's cat, Mickey, Tilly was also a victim, and never recovered from the attack. A coyote attack has an emotional and psychological effect on the pet owner, who goes through a grieving process. The first step in dealing with this grief is to accept what has happened, which can be difficult if you were not even

aware that coyotes had been living in your neighborhood. After all, we live in the city, not a national forest,
and we do not expect to see wildlife roaming our city
streets. It took me a week or two to accept the horrible
fact that a wild coyote had come into my neighborhood,
attacked and killed my cat, and then ate him less than
twenty yards from my garage.

Once I came to terms with that, feelings of guilt
swept over me like waves. I began to beat myself up,
thinking the outcome would have been different had
I made sure that Big Boy was locked inside the night
before—if I had, he would still be here today. Then I
began to feel like a bad pet owner, because a good pet
owner would never have allowed this to happen to a
beloved pet. Next I began to miss Big Boy, and I tried to
rationalize the attack by trying to rationalize a reason
for it. Most importantly, I thought of my other four cats.
How would I protect them from this coyote? A wave of
fear and anxiety swept over me as I contemplated this.
I knew very little about coyotes, and I had no idea what
I could do to protect my cats. I also felt I had no one to
whom I could turn for help with the coyote problem.

Despite my uncertainty, I knew I needed to act fast
in order to keep my other four cats safe. I had already
lost one cat to a coyote and was not going to lose another
one. I began searching the Internet for information
about coyotes. I had to visit many sites in order to obtain
the information I needed in order to coyote-proof my

fence, which ran along the common area of our complex, because not one site had all the information one would need for making an informed decision.[R1]

I remember finding one report on the Internet stating that coyotes avoided apartment, condominium, and townhome complexes due to the close proximity of such structures to people. As the coyote attacks increased, it was very clear to me that this was not true, at least not in my neighborhood. It appeared to me that the complete opposite was true; a coyote had found an ideal hunting ground with large concentrations of small prey (pets). I would add mobile home parks to the group above, as I have seen reports of coyotes attacking cats and dogs in multiple mobile home parks. In fact, the Sea Aira Mobile Home Estates in Huntington Beach, California, was located right next to a coyote den.[2]

One day when I opened my front door, I found two huge raccoons staring up at me. I slammed the door shut and just about had a meltdown right then and there. Now, not only did I have a coyote to worry about, but I also had two huge raccoons at my front door! It appeared as if someone had opened up the gates to the channel that runs behind my complex and invited all the wildlife in.

Two years earlier, our board members had planted trees along the fence bordering the channel in order to address resident complaints about the high noise level. The trees were planted to provide more privacy and reduce the echoing noise from our busy cross streets, Ellis Avenue and Brookhurst Street. The trees not only provided an effective sound barrier and more privacy for residents, but were much more attractive to look at than the channel. Our board members never once thought that by planting these trees along the channel they would be creating a new problem—providing a very private transportation corridor for wildlife.

In 2011, I was happy to find Carolyn Graf Matthews and Coyotes OC on Facebook. Carolyn was so patient with me and answered all of my questions about coyotes. If Carolyn did not immediately know the answer to a question, she researched and found the answer for me. In my community, we began to find cat remnants at the playground and in the pool area at the Clubhouse. Each week our groundskeeper or a contractor would find pet parts around my complex: the legs, tails, paws, and heads of cats. In the meantime, I was trying to find ways to keep the wildlife out of our community.

One evening when I was walking near the swimming pool area, a shaggy ground-hugging animal with a bushy tail ran right in front of me. I followed it, not knowing what it was. As I wondered what this strange creature could be, it began to zigzag and dart, and zigzag and dart again. I later learned that I had followed a fox that evening. (Coyotes normally run in straight lines, whereas foxes zigzag and run in circles.)

Every day, I was learning more about coyotes through my own research and with Carolyn's help. I decided to begin implementing some of the things I had learned. I periodically poured ammonia and white vinegar on my front and back patios and along my fence to reduce cat odor. I put pet food out for the strays only long enough for the cats to eat, and then I took the food back inside. The stray cats soon learned when breakfast and dinnertime were, so they always came by at meal time. I picked up pet compost from the common area to lessen the odor that would attract coyotes. I kept the cats inside at night so they would be safe.

The coyote attacks continued, and we kept finding cat parts in the common area of our complex. The playground was our biggest concern, because we did not want the children to see the cat remnants. We were also concerned that a child could be attacked by a coyote. We continued to post coyote warnings in our community newsletter. In July 2012 I ran into Judy Oswald, who was now a board member. Judy advised me that the board members had been waiting a year for the coyote to leave, and because the coyote was not leaving on its own, it was time we did something about it. I agreed with Judy—it was obvious that this coyote had no intention of leaving our community, which was an ideal small pet hunting ground.

I thought to myself, *If we can trap stray and feral cats, then we can certainly trap coyotes, too!* At the time, a coyote rescue group in Orange County was involved in relocating captured coyotes. All we had to do was capture the coyote in a live trap and have the group pick it up. Or we could capture the coyote and then deliver it still inside the live trap. Both Judy and I thought this was a great opportunity to remove our nuisance coyote! Of course, the live trap cage we were using for cats was much too small for coyotes, so I found a larger live trap in the *Recycler*, then drove to South Orange County to pick it up. It was an old, used, live trap about double the size of the one we used for cats—it was about three-and-a-half feet long and fifteen inches in diameter.

I began setting up the live trap in my condominium complex on weekends. I had researched trapping and learned that it was perfectly legal to set a live trap on private property. By this time, I had collected considerable information about coyotes, and even though Judy and I knew that old stinky chicken was the best bait to use, we decided to use fruit instead. Watermelon was our first choice, because we wanted to avoid trapping opossums and feral cats. Unfortunately, we still trapped one opossum and one feral cat, but minimizing the number to just one captured opossum and one feral cat was an amazing accomplishment, considering that this occurred over several months of trapping. The opossum was frightening looking, but not nearly as frightening as the feral cat. Each was released first thing when we found it the morning after it had been caught.

Judy contacted the coyote relocation group, only to find that they had stopped relocating coyotes. We were never given a reason why, and we were disappointed when we learned this. Now we were stuck about what we would do with a coyote if we managed to catch one. We discussed relocating the coyote ourselves, because I had a four-wheel-drive vehicle. But the thought of a wild coyote in my car did not sit well with me; I had a recurring vision of the coyote breaking free from the live trap and running around inside my car while I was driving. Sometimes the best decision to make is no decision at all and we decided we would just deal with the coyote once we caught it in the trap.

Every Friday and Saturday night, I put on gloves and carried that large, heavy live trap from my garage to the swimming pool area, placed it in the bushes, baited it, and set it. Then first thing every Saturday and Sunday morning, I put my gloves back on and went out to check the trap. I removed the bait from the live trap and then sprayed it with white vinegar and a water hose to reduce human odors. This went on for weeks, and though we continued to find cat remnants, we rarely saw the coyote that was frequenting our complex.

3

CHASING COYOTES

When deciding which tactical approach to deter coyotes will work best for you, remember that any plan will require a multipronged approach. The plan must incorporate several different techniques in order to be effective at deterring coyotes. Therefore, you should evaluate your situation and decide which method will work best for you. There's no single preventive measure that works on all coyotes.[3]

Like pets, coyotes have different personalities and respond differently to similar situations. Coyotes can be timid and shy. Coyotes are opportunists and will take advantage of any opportunity that comes their way. Coyotes are also very clever tricksters, and it is easy to underestimate them.

You can do many things to deter coyotes from your home besides pouring ammonia and white vinegar to reduce pet odor, picking up pet compost, and keeping pet food and water dishes inside. You should also make sure that all fruit is picked up, secure your trash can lid so coyotes cannot knock them over and get to their contents, remove bird feeders, install motion-activated lighting and sprinkler systems, increase the amount of outdoor lighting, and buy and use a number of great products designed to deter coyotes. Low-lying bushes should be removed, and bushes and trees should be cut back, in order to reduce the number of potential coyote hiding places.[R2]

Your objective is to create a hostile environment for the coyote by making your home and neighborhood coyote-unfriendly. Coyotes have a heightened sense of smell that they use as a hunting advantage. If a coyote walks past your home and smells pet odor, it is likely that the coyote will return and visit frequently, looking for an opportunity for an easy meal (your pet). People have difficulty understanding that if a coyote is frequenting their home, something in their yard or a neighbor's yard is attracting the coyote. Most times, the attractant is food, water, or pet odor (urine or compost).

Unfortunately, one's swimming pool cannot be removed, but pet food and water dishes, fallen fruit, trash, pet compost, and bird feeders—which attract birds and rodents—can be removed. Keep your trash stored in containers with locking lids, and try to keep those trash cans inside your garage instead of on the side of the house. Do not take your trash out to the street the night before your scheduled trash pickup day, but instead wait until early on the morning of trash pickup day to take it out to the street.

Look around your patio and your yard during the day and in the evening. Are there places for coyotes to hide and not be seen? If so, trim hedges or bushes to eliminate those hiding places, or remove low-lying bushes that might block your vision. Increase the outdoor lighting and install motion-activated lights. Remove woodpiles and other items large enough for a coyote to hide behind. Remove patio furniture, or move the patio furniture around your patio periodically so that your yard will look unfamiliar to the coyote if he frequents your home. You should not let a coyote become too familiar with your patio and yard.

If your home has a raised porch or foundation, walk its perimeter and close gaps or openings of 3 inches in diameter or more that a coyote could crawl under or squeeze through. This will also help keep vermin and other wildlife out. Periodically alternate the turn-on times of your sprinklers, or install motion-activated sprinklers so that coyotes will not get into the habit of being in your yard at the same time every day. Coyotes do not like water and will avoid sprinklers and hoses—both of these make great defensive tools if you encounter a coyote in your yard.

Many different products on the market are specifically designed to deter coyotes. Nite Guard manufactures a solar-powered, weatherproof, electronic device that emits a flashing red light. Simply hang the device at human eye level, periodically moving it to different locations in your yard, also at human eye level. This will create the impression that the Nite Guard is a moving predator (man) threat. One or more devices can be placed on your patio or in your yard, depending on the size of the area. I have had one hanging on my patio for more than a year now. Nite Guard also manufactures a reflective tape that makes noise and creates flashes of light when blowing in the wind. The sound and light flashes from the tape will frighten coyotes away.

You can purchase an electronic repeller device that plays recorded predator puma screams that will frighten away coyotes. The Yard Sentinel, a battery-operated ultrasonic repeller, emits a high-frequency 120-decibel sound blast to deter trespassers. As with the Nite Guard, it is a good idea to move these items about the yard, because we know that a nonmoving predator is not perceived as a threat by a coyote. You can also purchase wolf or bear urine to pour or sprinkle in small quantities along your fence once a week. Actually, the urine of male predators larger than a coyote (including man) will work, as the smell of the male hormone testosterone is what deters coyotes from one's home. As mentioned before, coyotes have a heightened sense of smell and will pick up the scent of urine placed in your yard. Wolf and bear urine can be bought in liquid or granule form, and some companies even manufacture synthetic wolf and bear urine that is just as effective as the real thing. The only drawback is that urine dissolves in water, so it must be reapplied after it rains.

The most effective coyote repeller is probably the Coyote Roller, which is installed atop a fence five feet tall or higher. The roller bars keep pets inside the yard, and they keep coyotes out by preventing them from gaining the footholds necessary to hoist themselves over the fence. The Coyote Roller needs to be installed along the entire perimeter of the yard, because as mentioned earlier, coyotes are very smart and will find the one unprotected gate or fence that gives them access to yards and pets. Installation of Coyote Rollers also requires the fence to be extended two feet below ground along the entire fence line, by installing an L-footer 8" to 18" below the soil and then covering it with soil so that coyotes cannot dig under the fence. Coyotes are avid diggers and can dig under an unprotected fence in a matter of minutes. It is also a good

idea to contact your city and HOA for building specifi-
cations and any special requirements before installing
the Coyote Roller.

Hazing is the method of using deterrents to move
an animal out of an area or discourage undesirable
behavior or activity. Hazing can help maintain coyotes' fear of humans and deter them from yards and
playgrounds. To haze a coyote:

- Raise your arms and wave them while
  approaching the coyote—be LOUD and LARGE!

- Use noisemakers (your voice, whistles,
  air horns, bells, and soda cans filled with
  pennies or dead batteries. If you have a pet,
  use your noisemaker in your home for a few
  weeks with your pet nearby to familiarize
  it with the noisemaker. Continue until your
  pet no longer reacts to the noise.

- Use projectiles (e.g., sticks, small rocks, cans,
  tennis balls, rubber balls).

- Try other repellents (such as hoses, water
  guns with vinegar water, spray bottles with
  vinegar water, pepper spray, bear repellent,
  and walking sticks).

- Sometimes coyotes will test you by pausing
  in their tracks and standing their ground,
  but continue hazing and chasing them until
  they leave the area and are out of sight.[R3]

Although you may not see immediate results from your hazing attempts, *any* hazing will help keep coyotes fearful of people.

Despite controversy among scientists regarding the effectiveness of hazing, its potential advantages far outweigh its disadvantages. Its advantages are that it keeps coyotes fearful of humans and it reduces habituation. In areas where people are reluctant to haze, coyotes are more habituated than in those areas where people haze. The more that people haze, the better the chances of keeping coyotes away from humans and reducing coyote/human conflict. Unfortunately, hazing is not always effective, especially with coyotes that have become overly habituated.

Some scientists believe that every time you feed or photograph a coyote, you kill that coyote. Each time you feed or photograph a coyote, you teach the coyote that humans are nothing to fear, which eventually leads to the coyote's euthanization by authorities when it is so fearless of humans (habituated) that it becomes a public safety threat. Once coyotes have lost their fear of humans, they cannot be retrained. So the next time you see a coyote, save that coyote by hazing him and keeping him fearful of humans; do not feed or photograph it. Something else to consider is that in parts of the United States and Canada where people can legally carry guns, it is not the gun itself, but the confidence a person gains by carrying the gun, that keeps coyotes fearful of humans. If carrying a golf club, walking stick, or baseball bat gives you the confidence needed to keep coyotes fearful of you, then by all means carry one.

Anytime a coyote is encountered, one should first determine if it is sick or injured and if a den may be nearby. Never corner a coyote, because it will only have one direction to go—toward you. If the coyote is very thin and appears to be losing fur, it may be suffering from sarcoptic mange (scabies). If you encounter a coyote acting aggressively (stalking, growling, biting, etc.) or with noticeable foaming at the mouth, it is likely to have rabies and should be reported to authorities.

Although I encourage people to haze and chase healthy coyotes, if the coyote is unwell, cornered, or limping, or if it may have a den nearby, chasing it is not a good idea. Instead, just back away from the coyote slowly, making eye contact the entire time until the coyote is out of sight. If you encounter a pack of coyotes, identify the leader of the pack, and either chase the leader or back away slowly while making eye contact with the leader the entire time. The other coyotes in the pack will follow their leader. After you have hazed coyotes in an area a few times, coyotes will start running as soon as they see you coming. Never turn your back on a coyote, and never run from one, because it may chase you. And most importantly, never show fear to a coyote.

Think of a coyote as a small child absorbing information like a sponge and learning from its experiences. Hazing is important because it keeps coyotes fearful of people, as they should be. For example, if a coyote sees people a few times with no negative feedback, the coyote learns that people are nothing to fear and becomes habituated. However, if a coyote encounters people a few times, and each time the coyote is hazed or chased, the coyote associates people with unpleasant experiences and learns to avoid and remain fearful of them. The good news is that if a coyote sees people and nothing happens, and then sees people and is hazed or chased, the hazing or chasing leaves a far more powerful impression than not being hazed or chased.

4

ONE, TWO, OR MORE COYOTES

My community has probably lost dozens of cats to coyotes since 2011, but I can recall only a few occasions when a coyote has actually been seen in our complex. Once, a neighbor saw a coyote run through the playground with a cat in its mouth. The resident said that the cat was already dead and he could do nothing for it, so he let the coyote have it. Another neighbor caught a coyote carrying his cat in its jaws, and he chased it into the channel until the coyote dropped his cat. My neighbor then picked up his cat, took her home, and held her in his arms until she died. One resident used to walk his dogs at 4:30 a.m. every day. He became the eyes of the community and kept us posted on his coyote sightings. He told me that once he watched two raccoons climb up a tree upon seeing a coyote coming their way. Even though the raccoons may have been a good match in a fight, they still feared and avoided coyotes.

On August 7, 2012, Blake Stair was with his girl-friend, walking his twin three-year-old girl dogs at the Huntington Beach Central Park nature reserve, when three coyotes appeared out of nowhere and snatched one of his two dogs, Chloe. Blake and his girlfriend had not been aware that coyotes lived in Huntington Beach until this tragic attack. A week later on August 14, 2012, the city of Huntington Beach had its first coyote work-shop in the Huntington Beach Central Park Library, where I heard Blake Stair speak about the incident and learned what had happened. Attending the work-shop were representatives from the Humane Society of the United States (HSUS), the Huntington Beach City Council, Orange County Animal Control (now called Orange County Animal Care), the California Department of Fish and Wildlife (CDFW), and the Huntington Beach Police Department (HBPD). It was at this workshop that I first learned about hazing—HSUS teaches coexistence with coyotes and the use of hazing techniques to keep coyotes fearful of people. This was also my first opportunity to receive information about coyotes directly from officials.

The presentation discussed coyote studies under way in Illinois and Colorado. Research was presented showing that when some coyotes are removed from a coyote population in a specific area, the female coyotes that remain begin reproducing at younger ages, having larger litters, and having more female pups. Within a year, not only have removed coyotes been replaced, but the number of coyotes is greater than before the removal. Also, when coyotes are removed, transient coyotes arrive to claim the vacated territories and home ranges. We were also told that coyotes are beneficial to the ecosystem because they control rodent populations. Many residents in attendance shared their coyote stories and voiced concerns about the coyote problem, but it seemed the authorities present were not listening. And although the presentation was informative, I remember leaving the meeting shaking my head and thinking to myself that these officials had no idea what was happening in our neighborhoods, nor a clue how large our growing coyote population had become.

All of the arguments for coexistence presented that evening are being challenged by scientists today. Most of the information about coyotes that supports the inverse relationship between population density and litter sizes resulted from 45 years of field research in Texas and Utah by Frederick F. Knowlton, PhD for the United States Department of Agriculture (USDA) between 1962 and 2007. In 1964, Dr. Knowlton started a field research station in San Antonio, Texas, and later a second in Logan, Utah, to study coyote population mechanics and the effects of coyote depredation on livestock and wildlife in rural areas. His work on coyotes and other species has had an extraordinary impact on the science and management of coyotes.

Logically, the argument that transient coyotes replace removed coyotes could be true, because today a greater number of coyotes inhabit fewer territories and home ranges than was the case in 2012. Some examples contradict the theory, however. In 1995, after seven coyote attacks in as many months, several coyotes were removed from Griffith Park in Los Angeles, California. Scientists found that coyotes living on the park's fringes did not move into the park, and Griffith Park remained problem-free for 9 years.[4]

Coyotes are part of nature's cleanup crew, as they remove roadkill whenever the opportunity arises; if coyotes are hungry enough, they will even remove their own. Although coyotes control some insect populations such as grasshoppers and cockroaches, the argument that urban coyotes control rodent populations is only partly true. At this time, urban coyotes control only mice and vole rodent populations, not rodent populations such as rats, despite what animal rights activists would have one believe. The argument that coyotes eat rats was disputed by Ohio State University biologist Stanley Gehrt in a television interview with Paul Caine of Chicago Tonight on March 26, 2015. Dr. Gehrt has studied urban coyotes for more than 15 years and has never documented coyotes eating city rats.[5]

Keeping in mind the adaptability of generalist coyotes, it is possible their diets could change in the future if they are forced to find new food sources.

Back at my condominium complex, we continued to set the live trap on weekends. Judy and I decided it would be easier to limit our trapping to weekends, in case we had to relocate a coyote—we both worked full time, so it was not feasible to trap and relocate during the week. I continued to pour ammonia and white vinegar to reduce pet odors. The groundskeeper was very good about keeping the pet compost picked up around the complex. Many stray and feral cats still roamed the neighborhood, but their numbers were dwindling. Up to this point, we believed that only one coyote was responsible for all of the attacks, because residents had never seen more than one.

In August 2012, Kyle Pheasant and Joe Vu of Fountain Valley, California, were disturbed to find a large puddle of dark blood on Vu's driveway. They followed the blood trail about 200 yards to the end of their Rock Fish Circle cul-de-sac and toward a green-belt that connected to Fulton Middle School. "I saw a pool of blood and I got scared, so I verified with my (surveillance) camera," Vu said. Vu's surveillance video showed two coyotes cornering and attacking Pheasant's three-year-old cat, Coco, and dragging her away.[6]

At least 91 coyote sightings were reported in Fountain Valley from January 1, 2012, through October 4, 2012. Nearly 40 percent were concentrated in the neighborhoods bordering Warner Avenue, Talbert Avenue, Newland Street, and Bushard Street. According to Lt. Kent Smirl of CDFW, increased coyote activity during this time was due to unseasonably warm weather.

Two weather patterns affect coyote activity and diet. Warm temperatures increase coyotes' metabolisms, thus making them more hungry and thirsty. Therefore, coyotes are more prevalent during warm temperatures as they spend more time hunting for food and looking for water. Likewise, when a storm front moves through an area, the increase in barometric pressure results in increased activity by coyotes. As with warm temperatures, coyotes become more visible after a storm has passed through and they begin to spend more time hunting and searching for water.

I remember reading a truism somewhere that if a person sees one coyote, another coyote is probably hiding nearby. On October 4, 2012, I learned firsthand how true that statement is. It was a Thursday morning, and I had the day off from work. I fed the cats as I usually do, and when I looked out my patio doors I saw that Orange was sitting on top of the fence. It was still early in the morning, and the sun was just beginning to rise. I went upstairs to change clothes in

my bedroom, which overlooks my patio, when I heard
a very strange sound. It was a muffled sound unlike
any I had ever heard before. I looked out my bedroom
window—Orange was no longer sitting on my fence
and was nowhere in sight.

I decided to investigate, quickly running down-
stairs and out my front door. When I ran around the
corner to the side of my house, I saw a large shadow
in the greenbelt beside my fence. When I focused
my eyes on the dark object I could see long pointed
ears, a snout, and what appeared to be a lifeless
animal hanging from its jaws. I knew right then that
it was a coyote, and that son of a bitch had a cat in its
mouth! I chased that coyote through the greenbelt,
down the alley, through a second greenbelt, across
the street, and to the channel fence all the way yelling, "Coyote, coyote, coyote!" As I stood at the fence,
one coyote approached from the north and turned
his head to look directly at me as he ran by. Then a
second coyote ran past right behind the first, head-
ing south down the channel toward Brookhurst
Street.

Neither coyote I saw in the channel that morning had a cat in its mouth, so I thought maybe the
cat was still alive and had somehow escaped the
coyote's jaws. I searched the entire distance that I
had run chasing the coyote, but never found a cat.
In fact, I saw no cats whatsoever, as they all went

into hiding. It was so quiet that you could hear a pin drop. The same phenomenon occurred after Big Boy was attacked by a coyote. When I returned home and Orange was nowhere to be found, my heart sank. Had I lost another cat to a coyote? I patiently waited, but after 3 days with no sign of Orange, I decided to throw away his cat box and dishes. The next evening I was watching TV in my recliner, when I looked out my patio doors and saw a great big golden fur ball. I could not believe my eyes—it was Orange! At first, I thought I was seeing a ghost cat when Orange returned home.

But we never saw Momma Kitty again, and I eventually realized that it had been Momma Kitty in the coyote's jaws that morning. At least three coyotes were hunting that morning, the coyote carrying Momma Kitty and the two others that I had seen. I originally thought we had just one resident coyote, but now I knew there were more.

These coyotes were conducting sweeps of our complex as part of their hunting routine. They would come out of the channel at one end of the complex, run through the entire complex as they hunted, and then return to the channel at the other end. Once I discovered how coyotes were entering our complex, I knew I had to step up our approach and incorporate the channel in our coyote-determent plan. I wondered how I

could make a channel coyote-unfriendly. I walked
the channel to get some ideas about what to do next,
and I talked with Judy, who was still an HOA board
member.

On October 11, 2012, a week after Momma Kitty
was carried away by a coyote, three teenagers were
returning home early in the morning less than a block
from my complex. One boy, who played high school
football and was more than six feet tall and weighed
over two hundred pounds, went out to his girlfriend's
car to help her unload it. His dog followed. When
they went back inside, they left the dog outside for a
few moments. Suddenly they heard the high-pitched
screams of their dog. One of the boys jumped over the
fence to rescue his dog, Freddie.

Both boys chased after four coyotes—two had
been on the driveway less than 10 feet from the front
door, while the other two had been standing guard at
the corner. One boy and the dog, Freddie, were injured
in the confrontation, resulting in hundreds of dollars
in medical and veterinary bills. The family had lived
in the area since the 1970s and had never known that
coyotes lived in Fountain Valley. The attack was caught
on a video surveillance camera and was later released
to *National Geographic*.

When coyotes attack their prey, they typically do
one of three things: (1) grab and try to shake their prey
to death as coyotes did with Freddie that morning,

(2) attack the neck region, either crushing the prey's voice box to silence it or severing the jugular vein to result in instant death, or (3) bite at the hindquarters, resulting in sudden blood loss that puts the prey in a state of shock and leaves it unable to move. Sometimes coyotes take turns chasing their prey to tire, weaken, and render it helpless. Coyotes may return to their den or pack to share their prey with others. Coyotes will normally eat the entire animal including the bones, leaving nothing behind unless they are interrupted while feeding or their attack is territorial or results from competition for space.

Now that we were certain that coyotes were coming into our complex through the channel, we asked Public Works to come out to see what could be done about the loose gates, all the fencing along the channel in disrepair, and other fencing that had lifted above ground so that animals could easily slide underneath. While walking the channel, I found plenty of scat, and I made sure that the scat found its way down into the water at the bottom of the channel. Scat is coyote compost; it is usually in a twisted cigar shape with a tapered (pinched) end and a much darker charcoal gray than dog droppings, which are usually brown. Normally one can see bone, berries, feathers, and fur in scat, which separates it from dog and other animal compost. Bone and berries are not so easy to identify, but fur and feathers (which cannot be digested) are very easy to see.

Although scat is used by coyotes for scent markers and to mark their territories, I honestly believe that urban coyotes leave scat to mark potential food sources as well. All the scat I have found has been strategically placed along the channel in areas with good hunting vantage points for coyotes, those spots where coyotes could see in several directions regardless of the time of day. Also, scat was found in the channel where squirrels were often seen and near the homes of residents who had pets. At a condominium complex near Adams Avenue in Huntington Beach, California, several resident pet owners found scat on their front porches. Until that time, coyote scat had gone unnoticed, because people never traveled the channel behind our complex, and the trees that lined the channel kept scat well hidden.

A representative from Public Works came out, investigated the channel, agreed to make repairs to the fencing, and asked the board members and me to clean up the channel and cut back overgrowth from the trees we had planted. I oversaw most of the trash pickup myself, throwing trash over the fence and then into large trash dumpsters. The board members had our landscaping company cut back all the trees inside the channel, and Public Works made the necessary fence repairs. All of this was done quickly over 2 weeks, and during that time we never found new scat in the channel. I believe this was because coyotes could pick up the scent of humans in the channel and therefore stayed away.

For exercise, I enjoy Rollerblading through the community on the weekends. While Rollerblading, I identified and followed coyote tracks within the complex, so I knew where and how coyotes traveled.

Coyote tracks and dog tracks are similar because both have four claw pads, but coyote paw prints are more elongated (oblong shaped and longer than they are wide), whereas dog paw prints are rounder. Coyotes also usually walk straighter lines than dogs do.[7]

Coyotes traveled along the channel fence inside the complex, then crossed the street in an open area, usually at a walkway or common area clearance, and then traveled between bushes and sides of buildings so they were less visible. Coyotes will travel the easiest path they find. This allows them to exert the least amount of energy while remaining as invisible as possible. Of course, there are exceptions, such as the few occasions when brazen coyotes ran right through the middle of our complex without making any effort to hide themselves.

Anytime I ran across dog or coyote scat in the complex, I tried to remove the scat for several reasons: (1) the coyote may be marking his territory, (2) the scent of the scat attracts more coyotes, and (3) coyote scat may contain roundworms or tapeworms. If you are a pet owner, probably the most unsettling discovery you will ever make is finding scat in your yard or on your porch. Scat should be removed immediately when found. However, you should always wear protective rubber gloves while handling scat, because you should not come into direct contact with coyote fecal matter, which may contain the eggs of parasites such as canine roundworms and tapeworms. Scientists are also taking a closer look at heartworm in coyotes. In dried coyote scat, heartworm eggs can easily become airborne, posing an unseen threat to people. Ingestion of these airborne eggs could make people seriously ill and could even be fatal. After scat has been removed, the next step is to pour or spray white vinegar or ammonia on porches, sidewalks, and driveways. White vinegar and ammonia reduce or remove the odor of scat as well as the odor that attracted the coyote there initially.

On Monday, November 19, 2012, the city of Huntington Beach had a coyote meeting at city hall. By this time, I was very concerned about the coyote problem in my neighborhood and about the safety of children when they played at our playground. When

Carolyn Graf Matthews asked for volunteer city representatives for Coyotes OC, I gladly stepped up and took Fountain Valley, because I had lived there most of my life. Carolyn decided that she would address the city of Huntington Beach at the city hall meeting. Another volunteer and I would address Costa Mesa and Fountain Valley at later dates. Carolyn addressed the mayor and city council, asking for coyote warning flyers to be mailed out with water bills and for warning signs to be hung in public parks.

The city of Fountain Valley had a city council meeting scheduled for Tuesday, November 20, 2012, and when I arrived I was advised that I could not discuss coyotes in the city council meeting, because they were not on the agenda. However, Mayor John Collins escorted me to the back offices and introduced me to City Manager Ray Kromer. Ray Kromer had been the city manager for more than 20 years, and he knew the history of Mile Square Regional Park and our coyotes. Ray told me that coyotes and foxes had lived together in Mile Square Regional Park for many years, and that coyotes fed on water hens known as American coots that had also lived in the park. When the American coots disappeared, the coyotes were forced to leave the park to find other food.

At first I found this information difficult to believe, because I had lived in Fountain Valley for most of my life and had even explored the storm drains and channels as a child, and I had never once seen a coyote or a fox. Ray reassured me that what he had said was all true—coyotes and foxes had always been in Mile Square Regional Park; they had just never had a reason to leave the park before.

Ray was surprised to learn that my community was experiencing coyote problems, until he realized that we had a channel running along the entire back of our complex. The first time I heard about channels as coyote transportation corridors was that evening when Ray said, "The channels are the coyote superhighways of the city." I asked Ray to insert coyote warning flyers in the water bills to warn people of coyotes in the city, and also to hang warning signs in parks. Ray asked me to review the coyote information already posted on the city website, and referred me to his assistant, Matt Mogensen, to discuss future concerns.

When I spoke with Judy Oswald, a board member for our HOA, she advised me that board elections were coming up soon, and suggested that I run for the board. I decided to follow her suggestion and volunteered myself as a candidate, even though I had never sat on a board before. I had already done much for my community in keeping coyotes out of our neighborhood, so it only made sense that I take a more active role in my community. Besides, I thought being on the board was a great idea because I would find out immediately about coyote problems in the complex, and that really appealed to me. So I ran for the board, was elected, and became secretary of the HOA. One of the first business decisions we made, in January 2013, was to increase the number of rat traps in our complex, because residents had been seeing an increased number of rats in common areas.

Later that month, the city of Fountain Valley mailed out a black-and-white coyote warning flyer in resident water bills. I was pleasantly surprised to see the flyer in my water bill, and I was happy too, because many residents were still not aware that coyotes were living in our city, which made them and their pets more vulnerable to coyote attacks. And even though coyote warning signs were never posted in the parks as we had requested, we were put at ease when we learned that all of the bushes had been removed from Mile Square Regional Park so that coyotes would have nowhere to hide. Another more colorful flyer was mailed out in June, resulting in greater resident awareness of coyotes. In the meantime, I sent Matt Mogensen a few emails asking for increased visibility of the coyote warning on the city website.

While visiting the Fountain Valley website, I realized that the city was asking residents to report coyote encounters to the Fountain Valley Police Department (FVPD). When I visited the FVPD website, I discovered their "Crime Trends and Analysis" section, which listed coyote sightings and attacks that had been reported to FVPD. Although very little information was provided about each encounter, there was enough for me to enter it into the Coyotes OC Google database. I also tracked report locations in order to determine the reporting districts where coyotes had been sighted. What I discovered was certain coyote hot spots throughout the city: (1) along the Fountain Valley and Talbert Channels, (2) along the Edison power lines parallel to Newland Street, and (3) to the east of Mile Square Regional Park.

At the same time, Huntington Beach released a beautiful four-color educational brochure on coyotes for its residents. Although the brochure was impressive, both Carolyn Graf Matthews and I believed it was missing some very important localized information about keeping Huntington Beach children safe from coyotes. However, we were happy that an effort was made to educate residents and that a beautiful brochure on coyotes was now available. We only wished that the brochure had been mailed with resident water bills so that more people could be informed that coyotes were living in their city.

By this time, I had already met Ron Shelton of Fountain Valley, California. Ron was the organizer of RD 43, a local group named after the police department's reporting district, which had been advocating the removal of coyotes in the city for more than a year. It was understandable why this neighborhood was experiencing coyote problems, because the Talbert Channel ran right through the neighborhood, while the freeway had many drainage ditches that ran along the back of the housing tract, allowing coyotes to travel freely and remain unseen. RD 43 was far ahead of most other Fountain Valley neighborhoods in keeping its pets safe from coyotes, and it was in direct contact with Lieutenant Kent Smirl of CDFW for questions and concerns about coyotes.

Back in 2012, few people reported coyote sightings and attacks to authorities for several reasons: (1) people did not want to get involved, (2) people did not want to take time from their busy schedules to report the information, (3) sometimes pet owners felt responsible for coyote attacks on their pets, (4) frustration by the general public that reporting a coyote sighting or incident is a waste of time because nothing will be done about it, and (5) reporting coyote sightings and attacks was an uncomfortable experience due to the overall attitude of those taking the reports. Because of resident reluctance to report coyote sightings and attacks, our tracker was designed to capture sightings and attacks not reported to authorities. Our original intent was to provide this uncaptured information to local police departments so that the information was recorded rather than being lost forever. Coyotes OC started its own tracker to encourage more people to report sighting and attack information, and to provide a more accurate picture of the coyote problem that existed in Orange County. I found sighting and attack information from several different data sources and entered it into the tracker, information that otherwise would have been lost. Now two new, strong sources of information were available to me: "Crime Trends and Analysis" and the exemplary neighborhood watch group, RD 43.

Unfortunately, due to budget cuts the FVPD only added coyote information to "Crime Trends and Analysis" up to April 2013. When I inquired about the missing coyote information, I was advised that information could be obtained directly through Animal Care Services (ACS). I continued to request these reports for several months through ACS; however, ACS provided even less information than the "Crime Trends and Analysis" report had, making it more difficult to track coyote sightings and attacks. Eventually, I no longer had to collect and enter the data on coyote sightings and attacks from ACS, because an increasing number of people were reporting coyote sightings and attacks. All the information I collected during this time proved valuable to me, because I discovered not only the coyote hot spots in Fountain Valley, but also a spike in coyote sightings in January 2013, with 31 incidents.

In the meantime, coyote attacks continued in my neighborhood, and we continued to find cat remnants. Yet we rarely saw coyotes. We continued to trap diligently, but it was like trying to trap ghosts, and we never knew for certain whether the trapping was helping and making a difference. Cats in the neighborhoods surrounding the Santa Ana River slowly disappeared. The people who lived along the Santa Ana River began to see less wildlife than before—raccoons, birds of all types, skunks, squirrels, lizards, rabbits, and foxes—and they became concerned that this wildlife might not return. They also began seeing more coyotes, mice, rats, and gophers in their neighborhoods.

Although coyote diets vary by region based on available food sources, our domesticated pets are easy prey for coyotes because they are naive about wildlife. When coyotes hunt for food, they cannot determine the differences among rabbits, squirrels, cats, dogs, and similar animals, and they see all small animals as potential prey. Cats are especially vulnerable to coyote attacks because of their small size and slower speed compared with those of coyotes. For the same reasons, small dogs are also vulnerable to coyote attacks.

For dog owners, coyote attacks of small dogs are much more common than attacks of large dogs. However, coyote attacks on large dogs have been on the rise as coyotes have become more habituated. These attacks are not predatory, but are territorially driven as coyotes defend their dens against other coyotes, foxes, and unfortunately, domestic dogs. Older dogs—as well as puppies—that are less able to defend themselves may be more susceptible to attack.

The number of attacks on dogs appears to rise during the late winter and spring coyote mating and breeding seasons. Coyotes establish and defend their territories aggressively at this time of year. Attacks on dogs can occur year-round, however. Most attacks happen at night, but pet owners should not put their pets out in the middle of the day, either. Remember, a coyote attack can happen anywhere and anytime, so always be on guard.

At times, our pets will know that coyotes are nearby before we do, because they can smell coyotes. I have read reports of pets that began to show signs of stress and fear, with their owners later discovering that a coyote had been nearby. Coyotes have a very foul smell (sometimes called stank) that I compare to the musty smell of a dirty channel. Even when coyotes are removed from the wild and placed in a captive environment such as a zoo, one can still smell the very strong odor of stank.

5

Early Signs of Habituation

Coyotes exhibited a marked change in behavior and increased aggression during 2013. They were becoming more habituated (less fearful of people), and it was becoming more apparent. Until the attack on Blake Stair's dog Chloe in Huntington Beach Central Park, the majority of coyote attacks were on cats. Now coyotes were beginning to attack small dogs. By the middle of the year, our greatest fear was realized when a toddler, in a cemetery with her mother nearby, was attacked and dragged by a coyote. By September, we were receiving numerous reports of coyotes chasing people. And by the end of the year, coyotes began to attack large dogs.

Coyotes are generally doing one of two things, sleeping or hunting. Naturally, coyotes are fearful of humans, and though they are normally out at all hours in rural areas, they have learned to avoid humans and traffic in urban areas by being nocturnal. Even so, it is not uncommon to see coyotes out during the daytime.

One must proceed with caution when a coyote is seen during daytime hours, though, because the coyote possibly is sick. Healthy coyotes are normally seen mostly in the evening when they are first beginning to hunt, and in the early morning hours when they are returning from an evening of hunting. Urban coyotes appear to be most active between 10:00 p.m. and 5:00 a.m., when most people are indoors or sleeping.

The January–February period is generally coyote breeding season, but coyotes may breed earlier in some areas. Coyotes are more active during breeding season, and weather patterns may affect and even increase coyote activity. Female coyotes become fertile between 1 and 2 years of age.

Coyote gestation lasts approximately 62 days— the coyote birthing season begins between mid-March and mid-April. Litters range in size from two to twelve depending on what the ecosystem will support. Some first-time coyote mothers may have smaller litters and may also have litters later than April.

The coyote pups are blind for the first 2 weeks and primarily stay inside their dens during that time. Once their eyes have opened, however, coyote pups begin to emerge from their dens, usually after only a few weeks.

This means that coyotes are more active during March and April, because they are hunting for themselves and their pups. Coyotes are also aggressively

protective of their pups during the coyote birthing season. If you ever encounter coyote pups, stay
far away from them no matter how adorable they
may appear to be, because their very protective and
aggressive parents will be nearby. One should be extra
diligent during March and April, keeping small children and pets away from possible den sites and safe
from coyotes. Small children should always be kept
within reach, and pets should be on short leashes
while outside, even when letting them out for only for
a moment to do their business.

Coyotes usually have more than one den. If
they feel threatened by a larger predator (man, fox,
or another coyote), they will move to another den. If
the current den becomes flea infested or full of scat
or urine, coyotes will also change dens. Dens are usually occupied only a few months out of the year. The
remainder of the year, coyotes can be found right out
in the open, where people can see them if they look
closely enough. Dens can take many forms and be
found in a variety of places. Dens can be found in
rocky areas, in sandy hillsides, under raised porches
or underneath houses, in thickets, under logs, under
woodpiles, inside hollow trees, and under sheds.
Coyotes will even find burrows made by other animals, dig to increase their size, and make them their
dens.

I thought coyotes had established dens in the storm drains, because I had seen them entering and exiting the channel through them. However, when I discussed this with Lt. Kent Smirl of CDFW, he advised me to look for concrete in the channels—coyotes like to burrow behind the concrete where they are protected. For example, a coyote den was found in the rocks at the Santa Ana River just south of the bike bridge between the cities of Huntington Beach and Costa Mesa.

Generally, dens face south, are on elevated land to avoid flooding, and have an opening that is usually 13 to 24 inches in diameter and about 3 feet long. The den may even have another smaller entrance or an air shaft.

By the beginning of summer, coyote activity in my neighborhood seemed to have ceased, and we were no longer finding pet remnants near the playground and swimming pool. Although we had never caught a coyote in the live trap, we believe it served as a threatening deterrent for coyotes, who eventually moved on to other neighborhoods. I choose to call the live trap an additional prong in a multipronged approach. The live trap alone would not have been as effective without all the other steps we took to make our neighborhood coyote unfriendly: repairing fences, trimming back trees and bushes, removing compost and food sources, increasing lighting, removing trash, reducing pet odor, cleaning up the channel, pouring wolf urine along channel gates, and warning residents to keep pets inside.

One Saturday morning I was retrieving the live trap, and although it had not been sprung, I found coyote scat next to it. I said to myself, "Well, I guess that coyote showed me!"

Another time, I found the trap had not been sprung, but a small animal, probably a mouse or rat, had left tiny bite marks in the fruit. When it was apparent that the live trap was no longer necessary, I finally retired it to my garage.

At Coyotes OC, we always dread July and August, because each year we see increased coyote activity during that time. Most times, coyote activity increases in August as nearly full-grown coyote pups begin to hunt with their parents.

In 2013, coyote activity started early, on July 18 at 3:15 p.m., at Forest Lawn Memorial Park cemetery in Cypress, while a mother and her daughter were visiting family gravesites.[8] Our worst fears were realized that day when a coyote attacked two-year-old Klarissa Barrera of Long Beach, biting her on the back and buttocks, grabbing her leg, and dragging her into the bushes. Klarissa's mother, Michelle Luper, was literally in a tug-of-war for Klarissa with the coyote, until Michelle screamed at the coyote, the coyote growled at her, and she was able to pull Klarissa away from it.

Klarissa was taken to the hospital and underwent a series of rabies shots. According to authorities, several coyotes were killed after the attack, and DNA was collected from each in order to test for a match with DNA the coyote had left on Klarissa's clothing.

What we did not see were news reports of DNA test results confirming whether the coyote responsible for the attack had been killed. Nor did we read or hear any news stories about the workers at the cemetery, who had reported to investigating officers that several coyotes were seen on cemetery grounds the day before the attack.

Regardless, the CDFW's quick action was effective, because no coyote attacks at Forest Lawn Memorial Park have been reported since the attack on Klarissa.

On September 13, 2013, the contracted security company for my community, Patrol One, reported to the current HOA board members—HOA president Carol Silva, Judy Oswald, and me—that at 2:30 a.m., their security officer saw a large pack of coyotes running through our complex.

Judy and I were aware that a black stray cat had been living in our complex's pool area. We had discussed trapping him, but when we learned of the pack sighting earlier that Friday morning, we realized that the situation had become more urgent and set the small live trap that same night to capture the stray. I went to Judy's place, picked up her live trap, and set it up in the pool area. The next morning, I was happy to see that I had been successful in trapping the stray. I then hung Found Cat signs all over the community in an effort to locate its owner. This cat was different—it was not a normal domestic cat, but also not a stray; it was definitely feral. As we expected, no one claimed the cat, so I adopted him, because by this time I only had one cat, Orange. I had lost three cats over the course of several months, two to old age and one to a brain aneurysm. Now there would be two: Orange and Zorro.

I would like to say that domesticating a one-year-old feral cat was an easy task, but it was not. A couple times I almost gave up, thinking maybe this cat would be better off with the coyotes. He was destroying my house and spraying all over everything, and I was exhausted. Somehow I toughed it out, though, and Zorro is a little less wild and much friendlier today. I believe that someone else in my community tried to domesticate Zorro before I captured him, but had failed. Like many other community residents had done with their cats, Zorro was released unneutered. I was amazed at how skilled he was at tree climbing. He would climb up the trunk of a tree to its top branches and then travel among the branches like a monkey. My neighbors and I agreed that Zorro's tree climbing skills may have saved him from the coyotes.

Once again, I pulled the large live trap out of my garage and set it up at the swimming pool. It appeared that this pack of coyotes had only been passing through, however, because we did not find any cat remnants or scat during this time. Even so, I thought it best to discourage coyote presence any way I could. One Friday night while I was setting the trap, a young girl asked me what I was doing. When I told her I was trying to discourage coyotes from coming into our complex, she confided that her family had lost three cats to coyotes. To be cautious, I continued setting up the live trap on weekends for several weeks, even though no new coyote incidents were reported. Although coyotes are much too clever to get caught in live traps, it appears that they do not like them and will steer clear of them, so they make great deterrents nonetheless.

At Coyotes OC, we continued receiving reports of coyote attacks on cats and dogs on our Google Wild Animal Tracking page, reports that we monitored on a daily basis. Carolyn Graf Matthews discovered an increase in reports of coyotes stalking and chasing people. She discovered that the reason people were being stalked and chased was because they were running from coyotes. A person should never run from a coyote, because that triggers its prey drive and will likely cause it to chase.

Three separate incidents occurred during just 34 days in 2013: August 3 at Laguna Niguel's La Vista Condominiums, August 18 at Huntington Beach's Magnolia Park, and September 6 on Domingo in Fullerton. We decided that the dangerous practice of running from coyotes needed to be addressed. We also received a report that a man was seen feeding coyotes from his van on more than one occasion at Isaac L. Sowers Middle School in Huntington Beach.

Some good-hearted people in our communities feed feral and stray cats. A feral cat colony exists in the city of Huntington Beach, California, and people go there daily to feed the feral and stray cats. What these well-meaning people do not realize is that they are attracting and indirectly feeding coyotes when they do this. As long as people continue to feed feral and stray cats, they will continue to attract more coyotes to the area.

Analysis of scat collected near Claremont, California, revealed that coyotes rely heavily on pets as a food source in winter and spring. At one location in Southern California, coyotes began relying on a colony of feral cats as a food source. Over time, coyotes killed most of the cats and then continued to eat the cat food placed at the site daily by citizens maintaining the cat colony. While authorities discourage the feeding of feral and stray cats, they recommend that if people choose to ignore that advice, all food and food dishes should be removed from the area after animals have been fed.

On October 4, 2013, we posted a warning on Facebook:

> We have just completed a review of the August and September coyote sighting data that were entered into the Coyotes OC tracking system. Thank you all for taking the time to provide this important information to us for tracking purposes. What we have discovered is an increased aggressiveness of coyotes toward humans. We have stories of people being stalked and chased by coyotes, which we have never before seen reported. (Remember to NEVER run from coyotes!) We also have a report of a man driving a white van feeding coyotes at Sowers Middle School in Huntington Beach. If you should see this man, do your part and either take photographs of the van or write down his license plate number and turn it over to the authorities. He is endangering the lives of the children.

Coyotes OC shares information about coyotes from all parts of the United States and Canada (except Hawaii, since it has no coyotes), because we want our readers to understand that coyote problems today are not confined to just a few isolated neighborhoods, and doing so allows us to see what is being done in other geographic regions to address coyote problems. Wildlife biologists believe that by doing so, Coyotes OC is negatively misrepresenting coyotes, because most information about urban coyotes in newspapers and similar media focuses on conflicts such as pet attacks. They add further that predators, including coyotes, serve important ecological functions, even in metropolitan areas.

The first report of a coyote attacking and killing a large dog, a nine-year-old great Dane named Zoe, occurred in Newington, Connecticut, in mid-September 2013 and provided a warning to large-dog owners everywhere.

On October 27, 2013, three-year-old Emeil Hawkins was reportedly bitten on the face by a coyote near Columbus Park in Chicago when he tried to feed it.[9] Although the bite Emeil sustained was later proven to be from a domestic dog and not a coyote, we learned from Emeil's incident that we must further educate small children about staying away from coyotes and unfamiliar dogs. This incident also alerted us to another problem with the reporting of coyote sightings and attacks—the inability of observers to properly identify coyotes.

We have received valuable research on coyotes from other areas such as Broomfield, Colorado, and Chicago, Illinois, and this research has allowed us to remain current on information about the highly adaptable and dynamic urban coyote. Broomfield has been a participant in the Denver Metro Area Coyote Behavior Study, led by Researcher Stewart Breck of the USDA-National Wildlife Research Center, since 2011. The Cook County Coyote Project is a comprehensive study of coyotes in the Chicago metropolitan area. Also known as Urban Coyote Research, the study was initiated in 2000 as a nonbiased attempt to address shortcomings in urban coyote ecology information and management. The Project is still under way and led by director Dr. Stanley Gehrt.

Recently, new research results from Urban Coyote Research has raised concerns about foxes as well. Foxes have coexisted with coyotes for decades. Although fox populations were not measured by researchers, during the 1990s when the coyote population increased in the Chicago area, the fox population likely declined (based on the results of more recently conducted research). This supports the general impressions of most nature center and park personnel in the area.[10] Some scientists believe that the decline in fox species is due to coyote depredation. Because the decline in fox species is a new discovery, scientists have not yet conducted sufficient research that would support the coyote depredation theory.

Another notable contribution by Urban Coyote Research is the Current Distribution & Historical Range map, which shows the progression of coyote range expansion throughout North America and Mexico. The historical range of coyotes prior to 1700 was restricted to the prairies and desert areas of Mexico and central North America. Since the 1700s, coyotes have dramatically expanded their range across North America, and now are found in an increasing number of cities in the United States and Canada. Coyote expansion has occurred in both North and Central America, though we receive very little information about coyotes from Central America.

*   *   *

By the beginning of 2014, I had once again retired the large live trap to my garage. Now that I was no longer trapping, I decided to focus on my secretary position with our HOA. As secretary, I was responsible for the newsletter, and I included coyote reminders in the newsletters whenever space permitted. Not only did these warnings protect our HOA from possible future coyote liability, but also they helped to ensure that all owners and renters in our neighborhood were aware of the possible presence of coyotes. One of the first business decisions we made as a board in January 2014 was to again increase the number of rat traps in our complex; residents reported seeing an increasing number of rats in the common area.

By this time, many community coyote groups had emerged on Facebook. One reader of Coyotes OC was inspired to start three similar community groups to provide valuable information about coyotes. The community groups supported one another, information was shared between the groups, and the number of members in these groups began to grow. What we found most interesting about people on social media was that they were quite open and willing to report coyote activity in online groups, but did not report that activity to their city police departments, ACS, or CDFW. Our biggest challenge was getting more people to report coyote sightings and attacks.

In early 2014, I was still collecting Fountain Valley coyote sighting information through that city's ACS. The January 2014 report showed a sudden decline in the number of coyote sightings and attacks—15 compared with 31 reported in January 2013. I was baffled; what could be the reason for the sharp decline? I was determined to find out.

First, I studied weather temperatures for January 2013 and January 2014. Finding that temperatures were similar in both months, I ruled out temperature change as the cause of decreased coyote activity in January 2014. However, I unexpectedly discovered that rainfall was considerably higher in 2013 than in 2014. I also found Mississippi State University research explaining increased coyote activity in January 2013. Researchers found that coyote activity, as for most wildlife, decreases during rain events but increases with barometric pressure. This suggests that coyote activity increases after storm fronts (warm or cold) have passed and barometric pressure begins to rise.[11]

Because the rainfall in January 2013 was heavy and in January 2014 was light, I was confident that I had found the cause of decreased coyote activity in January 2014.

After Houston, Texas, experienced heavy rains and flooding of its bayous during June 2015, residents began seeing coyotes running in their city streets and traveling along nature trails during daytime hours. Because the transportation corridors that coyotes normally used were flooded, they had to find other (unfortunately more visible) routes to travel the city. This was consistent with the belief that if rodents and other coyote prey were forced to move to higher ground during flooding, coyotes would naturally follow them. A storm front passing through is not the only cause of increased coyote activity. Increased temperatures increase coyote metabolisms, usually resulting in increased activity. Coyotes are also more active during the breeding season—the courting and mating stages especially are associated with increased activity.

Though coyote activity in Orange County, California, seemed off to a slow start in January 2014, it quickly gained momentum when the birthing season arrived. March and April are indicators of how active coyotes will be for the remainder of the year. In March 2014 we experienced a significant increase in coyote sightings, but coyote attacks did not increase proportionately. We later learned that 2014 had been one of the most active coyote years since 2010. Reported sightings to Coyotes OC increased from 155 in 2013 to 239 in 2014. Upon learning of this increase in coyote activity, we began warning residents to be extra careful in protecting themselves, their children, and their pets while outdoors.[R4]

April is normally an inactive month for coyotes—it is birthing season, and they are busy tending to their pups. Coyotes still must feed themselves and their pups, so coyote activity does not cease entirely. May 2014 coyote activity increased only slightly over that of April, according to the Coyotes OC tracker. An occurrence in Long Beach, California, however, was entirely unexpected.

Mark Hansel was sitting on a bench in Bixby Park, nodding off in the early morning hours, when he felt a strange sensation at his feet. "I looked over and noticed it was a coyote," said the man, who'd been homeless for a few months and had stopped at the park at about 2:00 a.m. that Wednesday while trying to figure out where he could stay. "He bit my socks; thank goodness it wasn't my toes," he said. "Then he backed off, but came back toward me." Hansel kicked and hooted at the animal until the coyote retreated and disappeared into a row of nearby apartments.[12]

Had Mark Hansel been awake before he felt the nipping at his socks, he might have seen the coyote circling him. This is what coyotes normally do when preparing to attack, sometimes approaching first to tug at the person's clothing or lick them. If you experience a coyote circling, tugging, or licking at you, it is important that you change the dynamics of the situation immediately, ideally by hazing and showing the coyote that you are bigger than he is. Either chase the coyote or back away slowly, looking it directly in the eyes until out of sight. Never turn and run from a coyote, because doing so invokes its predator/prey instinct.

Inherent differences can be seen between the sexes of wild animals including coyotes. Females naturally follow humans, whereas males naturally attack humans. If you can tell the difference and encounter a male animal, proceed with caution. Also, if an individual coyote shows an interest in you, asserting his dominance by making himself look big, putting his ears down, or showing his canine teeth, get the heck out of there, because that coyote is preparing to attack you!

People have actually tried to domesticate coyotes and make them their pets. All wild animals, including coyotes, raised by people as domestic pets are called charlies. Although charlies are more common and acceptable in rural areas, state and local laws make charlies illegal in most urban areas. Whenever charlies are found in urban areas, they are euthanized by authorities, because charlies are extremely habituated, unpredictable, and dangerous animals. Authorities consider charlies a public safety threat.

6

Coyote Meetings

In May 2014, we began seeing media reports about coyote problems in the city of Seal Beach, California. In one such report, coyotes entered the retirement community Leisure World through the flood control channels and attacked residents' pets. The problem had been ongoing for more than 6 months before the media began covering the story.

More than one-third of Seal Beach's population are senior citizens living at Leisure World. The remainder are mostly in their forties or fifties, educated, and successful. Some children live in Seal Beach, but it is not generally considered a young-family community.

In 2010 another retirement community, Rossmoor, located on unincorporated land near Leisure World and recognized as part of Los Alamitos, formed its own group of volunteers called the Rossmoor Predator Management Team. The Rossmoor Predator Management Team started a wildlife education program to teach residents how to deter coyotes from entering the community. Retirement communities such as Laguna Woods, Leisure World, Rossmoor, and Landmark in Orange County were especially vulnerable to coyote problems because coyotes easily identified elderly people as nonthreatening, just as they identify very old and young animals as easy prey. Even so, the majority of coyote attacks on humans have been of adults and not young children. Laguna Woods began having coyote problems as early as 2008, and has been trapping coyotes on and off since 2011. Seven coyotes were trapped and euthanized by the Laguna Beach Police Department as a way to control nuisance coyotes.[13]

Laguna Woods was not the only city in Orange County that was trapping prior to 2011. Others include Los Alamitos, Garden Grove, Yorba Linda, and Orange. Anaheim is among the cities that began trapping in or after 2011. City and county municipal codes and state laws govern the trapping and hunting of coyotes and differ by city and state. California state law prohibits the relocation of coyotes, explaining why the coyote group in Orange County stopped relocating coyotes in 2012. California Department of Fish and Wildlife Section 465(g)(1) states that animals trapped must be released on site or killed:

> Immediate Dispatch or Release. All fur-bearing and nongame mammals that are legal to trap must be immediately killed or released. Unless released, trapped animals shall be killed by shooting where local ordinances, landowners,

and safety permit. This regulation does not prohibit employees of federal, state, or local government from using chemical euthanasia to dispatch trapped animals.

Relocating coyotes is against the law in some states, especially under the following circumstances:

1. The coyote is only being relocated in order to move the problem to another city or town.
2. Relocation will be inhumane because the coyote will likely either be killed by coyotes in the territory to which it has been relocated or die trying to find its way back home.
3. Relocation may facilitate the spread of rabies and other diseases.

Before considering trapping, one should check city and county municipal codes and state laws. It is always safer to hire a professional trapper, who will already be familiar with local codes and laws. Hiring a trapper also reduces the chances of a pet getting caught in the trap. Another point to consider: some states prohibit the use of a weapon against a coyote, but the term "weapon" is so loosely defined that it includes everything from a slingshot to a vehicle (California Fish and Game Code Sections 3000–3012). Thus, hiring a professional reduces one's risk of being unwittingly charged with a crime.

Although it is against the law to use a weapon on a coyote in many cities, a person is less likely to be prosecuted for doing so in certain situations. According to animal attorney George Wallace of Wallace, Brown &

Schwartz, it depends upon one's location when a coyote is encountered. A person in their own yard, fearing for their life when a coyote approaches aggressively or attacks, and subsequently killing it in self-defense, would likely not be prosecuted by a court for wrongful injury or the use of a weapon. (If you ever find yourself in this scenario, it is a good idea to contact authorities immediately.) However, if one were to kill a coyote in a national forest or another area where coyotes are known to live, the courts are unlikely to be so forgiving.

Monday, May 19, 2014, was a very exciting day for all of us at Coyotes OC, as an ABC7 (KABC Los Angeles) helicopter news team shot video and snapped photographs of a coyote seemingly stuck on top of an eight-foot-tall block wall in a Huntington Beach, California, neighborhood. The coyote stood on the wall for three to four hours before it finally escaped. This was the first documented report of a coyote climbing a wall of such height by utilizing (perhaps) foliage, patio furniture, or a woodpile.[14]

Several stories of coyote attacks on pets circulated during summer 2014 as coyotes became bolder and began to enter the homes of senior citizens. Despite this unpleasant development, we also heard pet rescue stories that gave us hope.

The story that generated greatest interest was of a mother coyote that took her pup inside a resident's home to teach the pup how to hunt. This action indicated that coyote habituation had risen to a whole new level. Not only was the mother coyote so fearless of people that she entered a home to hunt for food, but she was also teaching her pup to have no fear of people and that it was normal to hunt for food inside human homes. Coyotes in Seal Beach had become so habituated that they were considered a public safety threat.

The reported number of coyote sightings and attacks in Seal Beach during 2014 varied from 45 to 60.[15] Regardless of what was reported, the actual number was likely 10 times larger. Unfortunately, very few people report coyote sightings and attacks.

Increased media attention given to Seal Beach coyote activity may have played a role in the greater number of reported sightings and attacks during 2014. The more that people hear about coyotes in the news, the more likely they are to report their own coyote sightings and attacks. A phenomenon known as reporter bias occurs when groups of people in certain areas are more likely to report sightings and attacks than are people in other areas. At first glance, it may appear as though those areas have a bigger coyote problem than others, but that is not necessarily true. The greater propensity to report coyote sightings and attacks tends to be found in locational clusters.

Another shortcoming in the reporting of coyote sightings and attacks is that some people are unable to properly identify whether a canine is a coyote or a dog.

Coyotes resemble German shepherds in many ways, but distinct differences exist between the two. Most notable are the wide, pointed ears, long narrow snout, and long skinny legs of the coyote from the front, and the long skinny legs and long bushy black- or white-tipped tail from behind.[R6] Because many people have difficulty identifying coyotes, they are either misidentified as dogs, or the sighting or attack is never reported due to uncertainty in identifying the animal. Even a fox can be misidentified as a coyote due to its big bushy tail. However, a fox is much shorter than a coyote and thus stands lower to the ground.

Coyotes have been known to crossbreed with other animals; the most successful pairing has been with the red wolf. The eastern coyote, also called a *coywolf*, lives predominantly in Canada and the northeastern United States. After wolves were hunted and killed in the northeastern United States, coyotes migrated north into Canada with minimal competition and conflict. By the 1980s, Canadian authorities were beginning to see a more aggressive coyote, smaller than a wolf but larger than a traditional coyote. Coyote aggression in Canada reached its peak in 2009, when Taylor Mitchell was killed by a pack of eastern coyotes in Cape Breton Highlands National Park. Eastern coyotes are now migrating south from Canada and down the East Coast, and eastern coyotes have reportedly been spotted in New York. The eastern coyote carries about one-third wolf genes, has a larger head than a typical coyote, and has eastern red wolf teeth with less space between them.

A less-successful hybrid occurs when coyotes and domestic dogs crossbreed. The more-aggressive domestic dog that results is known as a *coydog*. Normally, coydogs do not reproduce beyond the first generation, because they may be less fertile due to crossbreeding and the mating cycle does not coincide with that of coyotes. Coyotes are highly seasonal breeders and mate only once a year, whereas dogs generally breed twice a year. Therefore, one normally sees only first-generation coydogs without succeeding offspring.

Other types of coyote crossbreeding are rare and unlikely. Wolves, coyotes, and dogs all belong to the genus Canis and are thus closely related, while other species belong to different genera. Coyotes are too distantly related, not sharing enough genetic material, to interbreed with other canids.

On Monday, July 14, 2014, I attended my second coyote workshop at the public library on East Chapman in Orange, hosted by Lynsey White Dasher, director of wildlife for the HSUS.

Because the name of the workshop was "Solving Conflicts with Coyotes," I expected a different presentation from that in Huntington Beach the year before. Basically, it was the same presentation as I had seen in Huntington Beach, only with a much smaller audience. Though I saw many new faces at the Orange workshop, the stories we heard were similar to those that Huntington Beach residents had shared the year before. I did, however, enjoy seeing my favorite hazing video from the Aurora, Colorado, parks and recreation department again. It was at this meeting that I realized that coyote population growth was not limited to the cites of Fountain Valley and Huntington Beach, but was occurring in other Orange County cities as well.

Later in July, we were shocked to see a surveillance camera video of 46-year-old Nick Mendoza being chased by a pack of approximately twelve coyotes while walking his large Newfoundland dog in a Burbank, California, neighborhood. He tried running from the coyotes (something people should never do), and when that did not work, he threw lemons at them. It was not until Nick Mendoza climbed into his truck and flashed high beams at them that the pack decided to leave.[16] Mendoza and his dog were unharmed, fortunately. The whole incident was caught on camera, and the horrifying event was shown on the news for everyone to see.

August 5, 2014, was a very exciting day for all of us at Coyotes OC, as it was the day that Carolyn Graf Matthews rolled out our new Live Tracker. Now not only would all of our coyote information be available to everyone at any time, but users could search our database of coyote sightings and attacks using a number of variables, including zip code, city, street, and sighting and attack date, as far back as 2001. This enabled users to map the location of any particular sighting or attack with just the click of a mouse.

We were delighted with our new Live Tracker and knew that it was the first of its kind. By this time, we had received nearly four hundred reports, and our database continued to grow as more came in. Our prior Google tracker has been adopted by other communities throughout the United States to track coyote activity in their neighborhoods.

On July 26, 2014, a coyote burst through a closed screen door and into the sun-room of a Laguna Woods home, snatching a sleeping orange tabby cat named Cheeto. Jim Geissinger and his wife were in the living room about 20 feet away when they heard a commotion coming from the sun-room. Within five seconds, Jim Geissinger's 14-year-old cat, Cheeto, was gone.[17] This story is significant as a warning of the risks associated with open doors and pet doors. A closed screen door did not stop the coyote from entering a home and taking a pet, nor will an unlocked pet door. When coyotes first appeared in my neighborhood in 2011, I removed my pet door and never installed one again.[R5]

The coyote problem continued to grow in Seal Beach, and residents of Leisure World became more fearful of walking their dogs given the threat of a potential coyote encounter. Coyotes had become even more comfortable around humans, and in the middle of the day they could be seen roaming down city streets in the downtown area. On September 10, 2014, a forum was scheduled at McGaugh School in Seal Beach "where a coyote management tailored to the specific needs of Seal Beach will be formulated." A panel was formed with Mayor Deaton as moderator, representatives from CDFW, two biologists, and representatives from neighboring communities (who would report the outcomes of their coyote trapping efforts).

Many residents who attended the meeting shared stories of pets lost to coyotes and spoke about the growing coyote problem that existed in their small beach-town city. The panel listened to residents' stories, information provided by Lt. Kent Smirl of CDFW, and speakers from neighboring communities (including the Naval Weapons Station), ending by saying that a decision would be made in the near future and residents would be advised of the decision. Listening to comments from the guests invited to be on the panel, I discerned that Mayor Deaton and the city council were leaning toward trapping coyotes as a way to reinstill their fear of humans and to keep residents safe. Less than two weeks later on September 23, 2014, the Seal Beach city council voted to trap and kill coyotes.

I heard of the Seal Beach city council decision while I was on my way to another retirement community, Landmark, which is nestled in a residential area of southern Huntington Beach, California. It had been having coyote problems for some time when former California State Assembly member Allan Mansoor called a meeting to address resident concerns. In attendance at the meeting were HBPD Chief Robert Handy and the CDFW's Lt. Kent Smirl.

Residents lined up to share their stories, and one resident even brought a photograph he had taken of a coyote. Debates about claims of the large size of Huntington Beach coyotes had been ongoing, and authorities and animal rights activists believed the claims were exaggerated. This was understandable; because coyotes have long skinny legs and long fur, they look larger and heavier than they really are.

Lt. Smirl took one look at the photograph and said, "That coyote is fat! Someone is feeding your coyotes."

My first thought was of the man who had been seen feeding coyotes from the back of his white van at Sowers Middle School near Landmark, and considered the likelihood that Lt. Smirl's statement was true.

Landmark residents claimed that they were seeing coyotes at least every day and sometimes more frequently. They could be seen walking down sidewalks in the daytime. Coyotes had become so problematic that residents were concerned for their safety and that of their pets. When Chief Handy spoke, he stated that Landmark had reported only 18 coyote incidents that year, a number that the HBPD did not consider a coyote problem. We asked Landmark residents to be sure to report all coyote incidents from that point on, as it was obvious that only a fraction of sightings (7%) were being reported.

Thus, an alarming 93% of sightings and attacks had not been reported to authorities, supporting the more general belief that most coyote incidents are not reported. Meanwhile, members of groups on social media such as Facebook and Next Door claim that coyote sightings and attacks number are exaggerated, with the real numbers being far less. In response, I must say that quite the opposite is true based on the Landmark example and the magnitude of underreporting it indicates. This has been and continues to be an ongoing reporting problem throughout North America.

When people tell me that they have removed all coyote attractants, increased their outdoor lighting, put their outdoor lighting and sprinkler systems on motion-activated timers, and cut back all low-lying bushes and overgrown trees, but coyotes are still visiting their neighborhoods on a regular basis, I explain that sometimes their problem is locational, as they may be located near an oft-traveled coyote transportation corridor. Transportation corridors can arise from channels, rivers, barrancas, arroyos, schools, plant nurseries, parks, large open areas, golf courses, cemeteries, airports, and railroad tracks. Those living near any of these should be especially cautious when their families include small children and pets, because they are at greater risk of a coyote encounter. Those living near the aforementioned landmarks will see coyotes on a regular basis as they pass through while hunting for food.

This was the case with the Landmark community, and was magnified by building design and landscape bushes that provided easy places for coyotes to hide. A waterway to the west, the Huntington Beach Channel, feeds into the Huntington Beach wetlands and Ascon toxic dump site where coyotes live. A waterway to the east, the Talbert Channel, adjoins Sowers Park next to Sowers Middle School. Coyotes have been seen at the Ascon site and at nearby Edison Park, where they have stalked people who are walking their dogs.

Probably the most memorable coyote attack story emerging from Seal Beach during this time came from Vicki Young, who said her beloved dog was fatally attacked on September 1, 2014. "I haven't gotten over it and I'm not sure that I will, because she was my constant companion," said Young in describing the incident that occurred inside her Leisure World home after she had taken out the trash. "When I turned around, the coyote had her in his mouth and he was running out the door," she said. "She died. He ate her." By this time, many other pet owners who had lost their pets to coyotes could identify with Vicki Young's heart-wrenching words.[18]

In the first week of October, Coyotes OC began receiving coyote sighting reports from residents of the Huntington Continentals condominium complex near Brookhurst Street and Adams Avenue in Huntington Beach and less than a mile from the Landmark community. These reports indicated that coyotes were running through the complex and lounging on the grass in the common area at all hours of the day. One resident even provided a nighttime video of a coyote strolling down a street of the complex. Residents were concerned and afraid, and they asked that something be done to stop coyotes from coming into the complex. One resident stated:

> These coyotes are no longer afraid of hang-ing around the Huntington Continental condos . . . they are seen not only in early morning sightings but now even in the after-noon. Must we wait until a small child is hurt or found dead before some action is taken?

On Sunday, October 5, 2014, demonstrators at the Seal Beach Pier, organized by Empty Cages Los Angeles, protested against city officials who had approved the killing of coyotes in gas chambers. A pest control company named Critter Busters had been hired by the city of Seal Beach to catch coyotes in live traps and then transfer those coyotes into mobile chambers filled with carbon dioxide.[19] The protesters called the trapping and gassing of coyotes horrific and inhumane, and demanded a nonlethal plan to address the surge in coyote sightings and attacks. Conversely, residents who were afraid to walk their own dogs during the daytime and especially in the evening were also in attendance to support the decision by city officials.

For the last several years, an ongoing improvement and widening project has been under way at the Santa Ana River. It is designed to provide flood protection to the growing urban communities in Orange, Riverside, and San Bernardino Counties. The project begins at the headwater of Santa Ana River east of San Bernardino, extending to the mouth of the river at the Pacific Ocean between Newport Beach and Huntington Beach, covering an area of 75 miles.[20]

By October 11, 2014, the project had reached Yorktown Avenue in Huntington Beach. Orange County Public Works brought heavy vehicles and machinery down into the riverbed where they removed shrubbery, trees, and sand, and then poured concrete on the Santa Ana River floor.

Huntington Beach residents living along the Santa Ana River were aware of five to seven coyote dens in the area and knew that the dens would be displaced by the heavy vehicles, machinery, construction, and loud noise. However, they had no idea how this displacement of coyote dens would affect the neighborhoods surrounding theirs. Residents hoped that

Orange County Public Works would soon end the Santa Ana River Mainstem Project and spare them from potential wildlife conflicts. The project continued, though, making displacement of coyote dens in the area inevitable.

The Seal Beach city council met on October 13, 2014, and agreed to continue the euthanizing of coyotes despite protests from animal rights activists outside the council chamber doors.[21] A Native American played his drums and sang songs to protest the perceived inhumane treatment of the coyote, a mythological figure for most Native American tribes. Animal rights activists did not stop there; they took their protest to the next level by locating the traps Critter Buster had set and vandalizing them. Once again, residents of Seal Beach were in attendance to support the decision by the city council to euthanize the coyotes.

During this time, we began hearing stories from northern Huntington Beach about increased coyote sightings in neighborhoods just south of the Naval Weapons Station in Seal Beach. The trapping was definitely having an effect on coyotes as they began to move into nearby areas. By trapping, we were essentially moving coyotes from one city to another as had been done by other cities trapping at different times over the several years that had passed. However, we had no idea that Orange County Water District would soon begin a very large project that would have an even greater effect on coyote activity.

When Carolyn Graf Matthews and I learned of another coyote meeting being planned for the city of Seal Beach, we sent an email to Lynsey White Dasher, Director, Humane Wildlife Conflict Resolution, The HSUS, about our concerns regarding Seal Beach residents and their growing coyote problem. Many of the Seal Beach residents were either reluctant to haze coyotes (mostly out of fear), or physically unable to haze coyotes. In the email, we introduced ourselves and our nonprofit organization Coyotes OC provided information as to why we began our organization, and identified our mission statement to Lynsey White Dasher.[R7]

On December 2, 2014, the HSUS held another coyote meeting in Seal Beach, calling it a Coyote Deterrence Seminar. Despite the inclement weather, I drove in the rain to the North Seal Beach Senior Center. Only a small group of people attended. The seminar was basically the same as it had been at both the Huntington Beach and Orange meetings.

I thought the small turnout might give me a great opportunity to ask the one question I had been waiting to hear an answer to all this time. I mustered up the courage to ask, "What will happen once the coyote population grows so large, and the food source

becomes too small to sustain the coyote population?"
The answer was what I had expected to hear—coyotes
will starve, succumb to disease, and then slowly die
off. It will not be a sudden event but a slow and subtle
process, and you will not even notice the change in the
coyote population.

I returned home and reported what I had learned
to Carolyn Graff Matthews. This information put us at
our first crossroads with Coyotes OC. The main reason
why Carolyn Graff Matthews began Coyotes OC was
to find a solution to the coyote problem. Now we were
being told that the best solution to the coyote problem
was the natural one, to just let nature take care of the
problem: By allowing the process to run its course, the
coyote population will not rebound but die off naturally. And even though we have no idea how long the
process will take, we do know that coyotes will always
be here in the future, because not all coyotes will die
off in the process.

At this point, we were unsure whether we wanted
to continue Coyotes OC. But then we thought about all
the people who were still unaware that coyotes were
living in their neighborhoods, and we recognized
that those people could someday need a place to go
for information and to mourn the loss of their pets.
We decided to continue on with Coyotes OC, trying to
remain as neutral as possible on the subject of coyotes.

I needed to be certain that what I was told at the Seal Beach meeting was true, so I did some further research and found that by Charles Darwin's own account, his reading of Thomas Malthus was what stimulated him to develop his theory of natural selection. In *Essay on the Principle of Population*, Malthus argued that men, animals, and plants all tend to reproduce more offspring than nature can maintain. The inevitable result of this overpopulation is widespread death until the population is reduced to a level that nature can support. Darwin adopted this theory about the struggle for existence, and even made it the title of the third chapter of his book, On The Origin of Species, published in 1859. Modern computerized algorithms and predictive models can recreate field studies to support the findings of Malthus and Darwin from more than 150 years ago. In essence, we are witnessing this theory at work with coyotes today.

At the same time, the Orange County Water District began its Sunset Gap Monitoring Well Project in the Naval Weapons Station Seal Beach. Two wells would be destroyed in Huntington Beach, and six wells would be constructed in Seal Beach and Huntington Beach. Residents were warned to expect increased traffic, heavy equipment, trucks, and a drill rig in addition to noise, dust, and vibrations during construction. Residents near the Santa Ana River experienced all of these things during the Santa Ana River Mainstem

Project when several coyote dens were displaced. Now residents in the northern part of Huntington Beach would experience similar coyote den displacements.

On December 6, 2014, we began receiving reports of increased coyote activity from residents along the Santa Ana River. Coyote vocalizations in the form of yipping and howling could be heard along the river. By this time, Orange County Public Works had temporarily ceased construction in the Santa Ana River due to the weather. We began to see rainfall during the third week of December, resulting in even more coyote activity. Throughout 2013 we had heard stories of coyotes scaling residents' backyard block walls in search of food (our pets), but now photos were emerging of coyotes standing on top of block walls and peering into neighborhood backyards.

On Christmas day, Mayur Parnerkar fought off a coyote that had bitten his five-year-old son, Prathmesh Parnerkar, in Fremont, California, near Mission San Jose.[22] This attack was significant, because it was the first of several coyote attacks on young children in California. Whenever coyotes do something as aggressive as attacking a child, authorities are quick to assume that the coyote is rabid. However, most rabies tests on coyotes come back negative, leaving authorities without a good reason for the attack.

A coyote walks the channel adjacent
to a residential neighborhood in
Orange County, California

Coyote in a channel in Orange County, California

Another coyote in the channel

A coyote walks along the top of the fence at a residential pool.

Coyote
paw prints

Gopher holes

Coyote den

Coyote out for a stroll

Coyotes lounging about

Coyote close-up

Fence with angled apron

Our coyote
live trap

Coyote Roller
installed on a
chain link fence

Coyote Roller on
a masonry wall

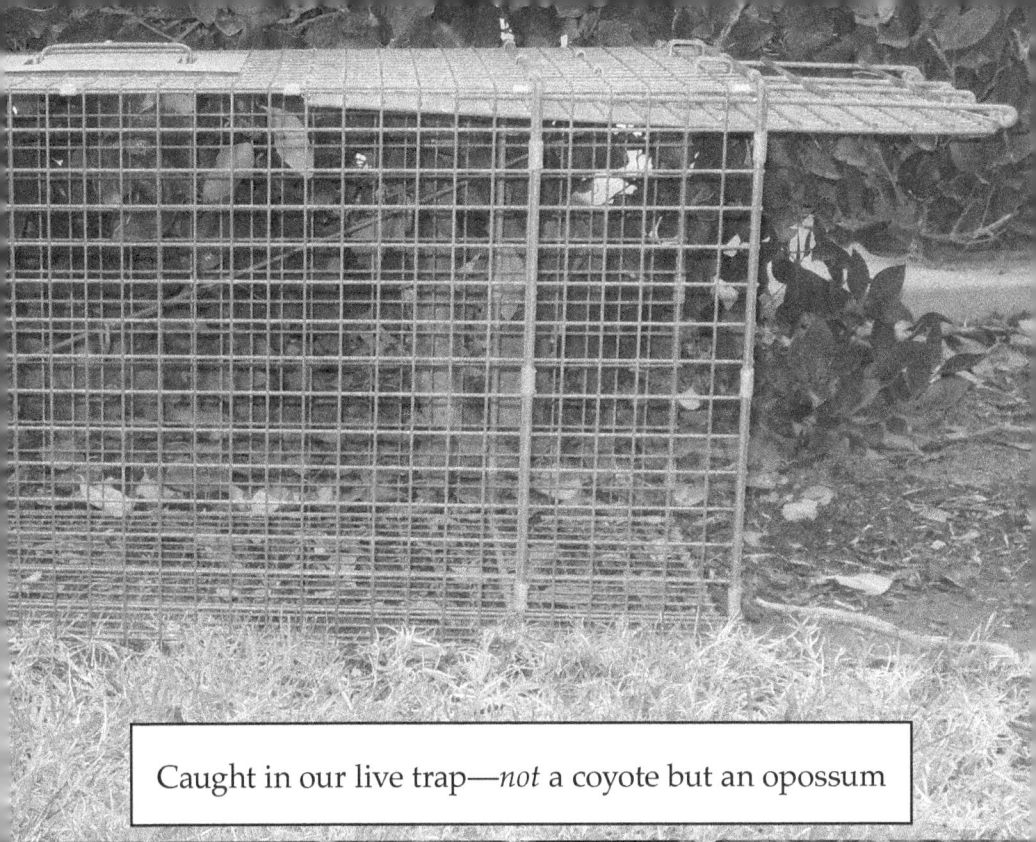

Caught in our live trap—*not* a coyote but an opossum

Tilly

Orange

Mickey

7

A Year of Changes

If asked what was most notable about 2015, I would reply that it was a year of change in the level of coyote aggression, notably with increased coyote attacks on small children in California. At Coyotes OC, we also saw increased computer hacking of and cyberattacks on our website. The majority of coyote attacks occurred in perimeter locations bordering undeveloped areas such as national forests. A few attacks occurred in heavily populated urban areas.

But first some history. It should be noted that the majority of coyote attacks have occurred within the last 10 years, and though many attacks have been reported, only two coyote-related human deaths have been recorded in North America to date.

On August 26, 1981, three-year-old Kelly Keen watched cartoons in the living room of her family's home in Glendale's Chevy Chase Canyon neighborhood while her mother Cathy did chores. Kelly wandered through the home's unlocked front door and stepped into the driveway, where she encountered a coyote. The coyote took Kelly in its mouth and then ran off, dragging her down the street. Her father, Robert, came quickly, chased the coyote off, and rushed Kelly to Glendale Adventist Medical Center. After four hours of surgery, she was pronounced dead, her death caused by a broken neck and blood loss that directly resulted from the coyote attack.

On October 27, 2009, an aspiring musician and environmentalist who enjoyed nature walks, Taylor Mitchell, went to Cape Breton Highlands National Park in Canada. It is uncertain what provoked the eastern coyotes in the park to attack—Mitchell's screams were heard by other hikers in the area, and she was later found with an eastern coyote standing over her. She was airlifted to Queen Elizabeth II Health Sciences Centre in critical condition from the extreme blood loss she had suffered. She died just after midnight with her mother at her side. Possible theories for the attack were that she was feeding the animals, disturbed a den, or tried to run away when the coyotes attacked.

Returning to 2015, on Monday, January 12 at 11:30 a.m., a coyote came out of the bushes in a Ladera Ranch, California, community and circled a mother and child before showing its teeth and lunging at them.

"It was terrifying, the fact that there's an animal out there looking at my daughter like she's prey," the mother said.[23] The woman was able to back away, and retreated into her house. The coyote went on to a neighbor's house and attacked two dogs, killing one and leaving the other so badly wounded that it had to be euthanized.

The new Live Tracker at Coyotes OC was a hit, and we received new reports of sightings and attacks daily. Of course, we experienced growing pains as our database became larger, and we were forced to continually upgrade and replace our servers. We experienced downtime between servers, but Carolyn Graf Matthews continued finding new, larger servers to bring us back online.

Back in my community, I no longer served as a board member for our HOA, because Coyotes OC required more of my time. A neighbor informed me that he had not seen any coyotes for some time, which was always good news. A few outdoor cats remained in our complex, but their numbers were dwindling. Though we no longer had a resident coyote, our community was at greater risk than others, because coyotes traveled the channel behind our community at night and in the early hours. Also, no new coyote reports had been received by our patrol service. However, this coyote-free peace became short-lived when two coyotes took up residence in the channel.

The life span of urban coyotes is similar to that of dogs—they normally live from 7 to 11 years in the wild and as long as 13 to 15 years in captivity. Coyotes have one litter per year with from two to twelve pups.

Coyotes look very much like German shepherds. Because they look like German shepherds, coyotes are often mistaken for them and vice versa. This is one of the biggest obstacles in obtaining accurate data about coyote activity and attacks.

The two canines differ, however, in mortality and detailed physical characteristics. The most common cause of death for coyotes is being hit by cars.[R8] As mentioned earlier, physical coyote identifiers include a head with a pointed snout and wide pointed ears; long, skinny legs; and a bushy tail with a black or white tip. Although a coyote resembles a medium-sized German shepherd, it weighs less than its domestic counterpart owing to its long legs and smaller abdomen.

Coyotes do not acknowledge property lines and the concept of trespassing, so we frequently remind people that having a backyard with a block wall or fence will not completely protect pets from coyotes. We ask that people keep a close eye on their pets while in their backyards and never leave their pets alone for even a minute. Due to the increased habituation we saw in coyote sighting and attack reports on our Live Tracker, we stepped up our warnings a notch in 2015 by asking people to always keep their dogs on short leashes when outside, even when taking them outside to do their business before bedtime.

The Coyotes OC Live Tracker received nearly two dozen reports of coyotes hiding in bushes; according to one report, four coyotes jumped from the bushes and attacked a Huntington Beach man's dog while he walked his two dogs to their evening potty break on Palm Avenue.

There is no such thing as a coyote-proof fence—a determined coyote will find ways under, over, or through walls and fences to get to prey. (Note: in the discussion that follows, "fence" is used to describe all fences, walls, and similar perimeter structures.)

Coyotes can be discouraged and redirected from coming through fences, however. For example, the Coyote Roller is a great, durable, long-lasting product designed to keep pets inside the yard and other animals out. Other less effective but less-expensive measures to secure fences include: clearing all bushes and vines away from the fence, as coyotes use natural elements like trees, vines, and shrubs as tools to get over walls and fences; blocking fence gaps that are 2 to 3 inches wide or larger; anchoring the fence by digging about 18 inches below the surface, placing an L-footer, and then burying it with soil so that the coyote cannot dig under the fence; and adding angled apron extensions to the top of the fence to make it taller and more difficult for coyotes to climb over.[R9]

Coyotes are avid climbers, diggers, and swimmers. They can hop a four-foot-tall fence without touching it. They can jump onto the top of a five- to seven-foot-tall fence and then make a single jump down to the other side. Coyotes can utilize foliage, patio furniture, and woodpiles to manipulate themselves to the top of walls that are eight feet high or even taller. A coyote can also dig under a fence in a matter of minutes.[R10]

In January 2015, we began to see growing signs that the rat populations in our cities were increasing. At first, I believed the growing rat problem was likely limited to my neighborhood because a channel filled with water ran along the whole back side of the complex. The more I talked with Orange County and Los Angeles residents, however, the more I realized that the problem existed in many areas and included rats, mice, and gophers. These areas had also experienced a heavy coyote presence according to reports from our Live Tracker.

By February, area residents began to notice more mice and rats roaming their neighborhoods. Residents also found themselves facing gopher problems and were calling exterminators to remove them from their yards, something they had never had to do before.

People found mice inside their pantries, eating anything they could find on the shelves. One resident opened her garage door one night to find hundreds of small mice scurrying about inside. Residents' yards were riddled with gopher holes. At night, residents saw countless rats running along electrical high wires and up and down trees.

Exterminators told us that business had never been better and that they were making a very lucrative living! At the same time, we were being told that coyotes benefit the ecosystem by controlling rat populations, and I wondered if it was only a coincidence that the four rattiest cities in the United States also had large coyote populations: Chicago, Los Angeles, Washington, D.C., and New York.[24]

Carolyn Graf Matthews and I learned that coyote diets vary from one area to the next depending upon available food sources. The diet of a coyote in California may be quite different from that of a coyote in Nebraska or New York. Coyotes, like humans, exhibit preferences in what they choose to eat. Of course, being an opportunist, if a coyote encounters prey while out hunting, even prey that may not be his first choice for a meal, he is likely to take advantage of the situation.

The dramatically reduced cat populations in our neighborhoods probably resulted in fewer true rodent predators, allowing the rodent population to grow even larger. The notion that coyotes control rodent populations may be true in rural areas, but it does not apply to urban areas today.

Let me elaborate further. Urban coyotes are quite different from rural coyotes and have evolved differently from their rural cousins. Available research supports the position that rural coyotes eat rats whereas urban coyotes do not. Coyotes are generalists and highly adaptive when it comes to finding food, so it is possible that if their food sources were to become scarce, urban coyotes would adapt by adding rats to their diets as their rural cousins have done. Currently, however, rats are not included in the urban coyote's diet. The typical coyote diet consists of cockroaches, grasshoppers, berries, fruit, mice, voles, rabbits, gophers, squirrels, raccoons, and birds (along with their eggs).

On March 26, 2015, we received answers to many urban coyote questions when Paul Caine from the television program Chicago Tonight interviewed Dr. Stanley Gehrt, a biologist for Ohio State University. Dr. Gehrt indicated that Urban Coyote Research, which was formed in 2000, had not documented the eating of city rats by urban coyotes. Although Carolyn and I already knew that urban coyotes had adapted and evolved differently from their rural cousins, Dr. Gehrt affirmed our preconceptions in his interview.

Dr. Gehrt discussed other differences between urban and rural coyotes in addition to rats not being part of the urban coyote diet:

- Both reproductive and survival rates are higher for urban coyotes than they are for rural coyotes.

- Litter sizes of urban coyotes are nearly double those of rural coyotes.

- Urban coyotes are primarily nocturnal, whereas rural coyotes can be either nocturnal or diurnal depending upon their individual personalities.

In addition, urban coyotes live longer than rural coyotes—from 7 to 11 years, and as long 15 years in captivity, whereas rural coyotes usually live less than 3 years. Dr. Gehrt indicated that this is because trapping and hunting of rural coyotes does not occur in urban cities (with the exception of trapping by government agencies), and people are more efficient at removing coyotes with guns in rural areas than at removing coyotes with vehicles in urban cities.[25]

A question not asked of Dr. Gehrt in the interview was why urban coyotes would be attacking and killing cats and dogs if an abundance of natural food was available to them. Squirrel, gopher, and bird populations were thriving in urban cities. I also wondered why only the danger that coyotes present for dogs was discussed, while the danger that coyotes pose for cats was never addressed.

I understand that a coyote cannot differentiate between a rabbit and a cat, so it sees a cat as prey. It is also clear to me that a coyote sees a dog as competition (and maybe even a threat), and a coyote's natural instinct is to remove the competition (or threat), and this happens more often during coyote courting and breeding season. Based on reports from our Live Tracker at Coyotes OC, the number of coyote attacks on cats is nearly equal to that of coyote attacks on dogs. Even so, these numbers may be misleading, because when a cat disappears, its owner often believes that it just wandered off. And unlike dogs, cats rarely survive coyote attacks. As a result, many cat disappearances are never reported.

In the end, probably the most important point made by Dr. Gehrt during the interview was, "Please do not feed coyotes!"

In addition to the coyote breeding and birthing seasons is a phase known as coyote dispersal. Coyote dispersal season mostly affects juvenile coyotes (less than one year old), beginning in October and lasting through February, and is the phase when coyotes leave their homes and venture out to find their own territories or home ranges. A juvenile coyote can disperse either within a group or as a solitary transient. Chances of survival are greater for those that disperse within a group.

Some coyotes remain at home to help their parents and do not disperse until their second year. Little is known about juvenile coyotes, and why some disperse immediately while others stay behind. Likewise, little is known about the length of time it can take to complete the dispersal process. Coyotes may disperse up to 100 miles in their search for a new home.

When I saw the photograph of a coyote on a rooftop in Queens, New York, in the news on March 30, 2015, my first question was, "How did the coyote get on top of the roof?" I never thought to ask where the coyote had come from. I also did not realize that it might be a juvenile. The coyote entered an old vacant warehouse next door to the L.I.C. Bar, then climbed up to the roof, jumped through an open window, and made its way next door to the rooftop where it was spotted. The owner of the L.I.C. Bar, Brian Porter, stated, "He escaped two police officers, and he jumped on the roof adjacent to me and then jumped through the window of the vacant building.[26] The elusive Queens coyote was not captured until April 28, 2015.

In the meantime, a different coyote made its way into Midtown Manhattan. On April 14, a coyote in Chelsea led NYPD officers on a wild chase until it was finally contained and shot with tranquilizer darts. The coyote was taken to the American Society for the Prevention of Cruelty to Animals for a checkup and to Animal Care and Control. The coyote was collared and later released in the Bronx. However, residents were left with a question: how does a coyote end up in the middle of Manhattan? Experts believed the Chelsea coyote easily could have migrated from Connecticut or Westchester County.

The coyote problem during this time was not only in New York, but also in New Jersey. On April 19, an aggressive coyote bit a Norwood man on his leg while the man was out walking his dog. The following day, a coyote chewed the tires of a Norwood Police Department patrol car on Villa Court behind Norwood Public School. Two dens were discovered near the school, and all outdoor gym, recess, and after-school activities were canceled when a coyote was spotted on school grounds.[27] Two days later, state health officials announced that an aggressive coyote, shot and killed in the borough after it attacked a police car, had tested positive for rabies.

On April 23, a coyote was spotted on Manhattan's Upper West Side near West End Avenue. Officers searched for the coyote by patrol car, on foot, on horseback, and with a helicopter, but the coyote eluded them. Riverside Park was kept open during the entire ordeal. The Hudson River runs along Riverside Park and travels north into less developed areas, making the Hudson River a perfect travel corridor for coyotes.

On April 24, New York City was still experiencing coyote problems, and officers of the NYPD were now in pursuit of a coyote in Battery Park City. This chase was more dramatic, as police followed a running coyote in squad cars with lights flashing. All of this was caught on camera and shared on news stations. Eventually, the coyote was cornered in the outdoor seating area of a café, where officials took aim with a CO2-powered rifle and shot the animal with a Ketaset-filled tranquilizing dart. The coyote captured at the café was nicknamed the Cappuccino Coyote.

During all the coyote activity in March and April in New York City, residents were perplexed as to why a slew of coyotes had descended on their city. Wildlife biologist Chris Nagy later explained that young coyotes traveled south down the green-park corridors hugging the Hudson River in search of homes, and the migration could become a seasonal event. Long Island (which includes Queens) did not yet have a coyote breeding population, but when a coyote was seen on Long Island on April 25, researchers agreed that such a development was inevitable. Meanwhile, juvenile coyotes continued to appear in the city, and the NYPD continued to tranquilize them, capture them, and return them to the Bronx.

The following day in Newton County, Georgia, a family found a coyote sitting on their kitchen counter. Apparently, Newton County had been experiencing growth in its coyote population. Animal control officers said that coyote complaints were up in both Rockdale and Newton Counties. The photograph of the coyote sitting on their kitchen counter is quite surprising, and it appears as though the coyote is looking up at the photographer and saying, "What's for lunch?"

Another coyote sighting occurred in New York City on May 7, 2015, this time near LaGuardia Airport. A coyote lurked just a few hundred yards from a major runway, and a letter carrier spotted it in a marsh near Ditmars Boulevard and 78th Street in East Elmhurst at around 2:00 a.m., according to Port Authority police. But when the police tried to wrangle it, the critter darted north to Elmjack Field and got away.[28] It was the latest in a string of coyote sightings around the city.

While the East Coast was dealing with its coyote problems, we were experiencing our own in California.

On April 22, the Coyotes OC website was brought down by hackers. Although Carolyn Graf Matthews and I suspected animal rights activists, we had no way of proving our suspicion. We discussed our options and even considered setting traps on the website to catch the culprits in the act.

By this time, other cities in the United States were setting up Google trackers like the one we started in 2011 to track residents' coyote sightings and attacks.

Tracking coyote activity allows residents to be proactive with coyote problems in their neighborhoods. Tracking provides the necessary information to identify coyote hot spots and allows residents to focus hazing and cleanup efforts in those areas. Sometimes simply removing trash and cutting back overgrown bushes and trees can make an area less attractive to coyotes. Bringing a volunteer hazing team into the area a few times also helps discourage coyotes from returning.

On May 5, we experienced more growing pains at Coyotes OC when our site went down again. This time our drive was full—we had outgrown our server. Carolyn Graf Matthews secured another server, and we were up and running again in no time. The Live Tracker that Carolyn had created was proving to be quite an effective tool in capturing coyote sightings and attacks that might otherwise have been lost.

The first coyote attack on a child in Irvine, California, occurred at 6:00 p.m. on May 22 when a coyote lunged at a three-year-old girl playing with her twin sister in Silverado Park. The park is located at Silverado and Equinox in a newly developed area in the northeastern part of the city. The neighborhood is identified as a perimeter area because it is just south of the 241 Highway near Limestone Canyon Regional Park.

The girl was taken to a hospital and released a few hours later with a minor cut on her neck. Fish & game and animal control officers with the Irvine Police Department continued to look for the coyote. Police said that although coyotes frequented the area, it was extremely rare for one to attack a person.

A couple days later, a Huntington Beach resident contacted me and asked if I knew that foxes were living near the Santa Ana River. A friend had been walking his dog along the nature trail when something came up from behind him and snatched his dog right off its leash, taking off and leaving behind only the leash. The friend was certain that the culprit was a fox. It had been more than 3 years since I had seen a fox and a couple years since I had last heard of one being seen. I told the resident I had not heard of foxes being in the area, and quite frankly, I thought coyotes had removed all foxes from the cities of Fountain Valley and Huntington Beach. (Six months later, workers at a plant nursery located along the Santa Ana River at Adams Avenue confirmed that a fox was living in the nursery.)

On June 12, 2015, I heard that our HOA president, Carol Silva, had opened her front door to take her dog outside for a walk at 6:30 p.m. only to have a coyote run up to her and her dog. Carol remembered everything I had written in the newsletter about coyotes and quickly pulled on the leash, bringing her dog toward her and putting it inside the house. Carol handled

the encounter like a professional. Her quick thinking probably saved her dog's life. It had been months
since we had seen coyotes in our complex, and now
Carol had one right at her front door in broad daylight!
When I saw Carol almost two weeks later, she showed
me the direction from which the coyote had come and
asked me to go into the channel to check for evidence
of coyote activity. I agreed to do so in order to put her
mind at ease.

On June 23, 2015, a two-year-old child was bitten
on the knee and his leg was bruised by a coyote
while near a playground on Borrego, a street in Irvine
less than one mile from where the first attack had
occurred. Although the injuries were minor, authorities were now becoming concerned about the recent
attacks on small children. Though very little information was provided to the media at the time, authorities
were searching for and euthanizing coyotes in the
area where the attacks had occurred. The Irvine Police
Department and CDFW officers were doing all they
could to bring the growing coyote problem under control, which was believed to be the result of the drought
and subsequent lack of food and water.

It was not until June 24, 2015, that I finally returned
to Ellis Avenue, entering the channel through the gate
as I had done many times before. While walking the
channel, I remembered walking it in 2011 after Big
Boy's attack and seeing scat all over the bank of the

channel. As I walked the length of the channel, a big smile grew on my face as I realized that no scat was evident this time. When I finally reached the bend and could see Brookhurst Street in the distance, I ran across something on the ground. My smile faded—it was a pile of scat!

I yelled and kicked the scat, and it fell down into the bushes on the floor of the channel. Suddenly, a coyote jumped out of the bushes in the channel below and took off running. I was so startled that I went into "fight" mode and chased it all the way down the channel, under the Brookhurst bridge, and beyond. The coyote had been sleeping in the bushes at the bottom of the channel where it had a direct line to Carol's house. I could tell that the coyote was young, as he still had a baby face.

This coyote was likely trying to make the channel behind our complex his new home range or territory. I went to Carol's house and reported what I had found, and we agreed that we needed to get the coyote out of the channel. Carol also asked me to report all coyote sightings to the FVPD, as she wanted a record of all the coyote activity in our neighborhood. At the time, we had no idea that a number of coyote sightings would be reported to the FVPD during the five months that would follow.

On June 26, 2015, I walked the channel again, looking for coyotes. What I saw pulled the rug right out from under me. Not just one coyote was in the channel this time, but two! I chased them down the channel all the way to the other side of Brookhurst Street. I was not happy about this—my first thought was that it could be a mating pair with a den in the channel. This would mean our problems were much larger than I had originally thought. Once again, I visited Carol, advised her about what I had seen, and called the FVPD to report the sighting. I did not tell Carol about my concern that the coyotes might be a mating pair.

I decided to return to the channel every night, hazing coyotes every time I saw them (schedule permitting) until I had chased them out for good. I thought to myself, How hard could it be?

I returned to the channel nightly with my bat, chasing the coyotes and yelling and screaming. I estimated that it would take a few weeks to convince them to leave. This was all new territory for me, as I had never before used hazing as a way to persuade coyotes to move out of an area. In retrospect, I obviously underestimated the coyotes, because they made it perfectly clear to me that they had no intention of leaving the channel.

On June 28, I saw a coyote in the channel near the bend at Sparrow Avenue. I also discovered that coyotes were sliding under the chain link fence in two areas of Sparrow Avenue, so I spoke with local residents about it. I found that cats were missing, and coyotes had been seen at the front doors of homes on Sparrow Avenue! One resident even told me that she had recently seen four coyotes wandering together down Sparrow Avenue and had reported them to the FVPD.

The thought of four coyotes roaming the streets of our complex sent chills down my spine. I remember wondering what would be worse: a mating pair living in the channel, or four coyotes roaming the streets of our complex? Either way, this was not good news for residents whose homes backed up to the channel or who lived in areas nearby. A week passed; I did not see any coyotes and thought that maybe they had finally moved on.

Then on July 5, 2015, I returned to the channel and found two coyotes again! I was disappointed that they were back, but I would not let that discourage me—I was determined to stick with my plan. Once again, I chased the coyotes down the channel, hoping that this would be the last time I ever saw them. By this time, I realized that my plan would take longer than I had anticipated. My question to myself was, How long will it take to convince these coyotes to leave?

8

MORE COYOTE ATTACKS ON CHILDREN

That same day, July 5, two more children had encounters with coyotes in Irvine, with a coyote entering a garage each time. One incident was considered an attack, because a two-and-a-half-year-old boy was bitten several times in his family's garage on Keepsake near Portola Parkway, not far from where the first two attacks on small children had occurred. The second incident was technically not considered an attack, because a seven-year-old girl was scratched by a coyote but not bitten. This incident occurred farther south at a nonperimeter, more central location of Irvine on Denim near Irvine Boulevard. The coyote entered the garage and then the home through an open door. I cannot emphasize enough how important it is to always keep windows and doors closed, as coyotes have been known to enter homes through them. Coyotes do not observe boundaries and will readily cross them if a good opportunity presents itself.

The pup rearing season lasts from March through August—July and August are the most active months, and we were only in the first week of that busy period. By July 9, five coyotes had been euthanized in Irvine, the city taking a more aggressive approach because the first coyote attack had been on a small child. Only one of the euthanized coyotes could be matched by DNA and was linked to just one attack. Authorities were not done trapping and euthanizing of coyotes yet, however; the final results of their efforts would not be known until November.

Officials are sometimes able to identify a nuisance coyote, once captured, through DNA testing. In order for DNA testing to be effective, however, officials need a good DNA sample in terms of quality and size. If the sample is not clean or is too small to test, results can be inconclusive. Several nuisance coyotes have been identified through DNA testing after being euthanized, but many other DNA tests have been inconclusive. And in some instances, authorities have euthanized a number of coyotes only to later disclose that none were DNA matches to the nuisance coyote being sought.

During the period when the Irvine coyote attacks on children occurred, Carolyn Graf Matthews and I discovered that many parents were not teaching their children what to do if they saw a coyote or an unfamiliar dog. A small child is unlikely to be able to distinguish a coyote from a dog, but it is best to show children photos of both so that they learn to recognize features of either animal. Children should also be taught that if they see a coyote or dog they do not know, they should back away from the animal very slowly, looking it in the eyes the entire time until the animal can no longer be seen. Once the animal is gone, the child should either find an adult or return home immediately. Children should also be advised that if the animal does not leave, they should scream and wave their hands above their head to scare the coyote. If the animal still does not leave, children should pick up rocks or anything similar that they can find nearby and throw them at the coyote or dog. Most important, children should be told never to run from a coyote or dog.[R10]

Back in the channel behind my complex, a single coyote gave me a workout when I chased him down the channel past Brookhurst Street on both July 7 and July 8. Several days passed, and I began to think that I had finally succeeded in chasing all the coyotes out of the channel for good. Then on July 13, another coyote appeared in the channel. As I had with the others before it, I chased the coyote as far as I could down the channel toward Brookhurst Street.

I started to believe that these coyotes were testing me. They would leave for a short time but return a few days later. On this particular day, two neighbors popped their heads over their backyard block walls, and I stopped to talk with them. I let them know that I had found two coyotes living in the channel in June, and that our board members had decided it was best that we persuade the coyotes to leave, because allowing them to stay would only lead to bigger problems later on. I could just picture two adult coyotes and several coyote pups running around the channel as I was telling my neighbors this. Their backyards ran along the channel, but they had no idea that coyotes had been living there for a month or longer.

As tedious as it could be to walk the channel every day, hazing coyotes every time I saw them, I learned more about them during this process. The first time I saw coyotes in the channel after Momma Kitty had been carried off, they were running along the channel bank. I began to put down wolf urine, and later bear urine, at the gates of the channel to keep coyotes from exiting the channel and entering our complex to hunt.

Also while hazing, I learned how unpredictable coyotes are. A couple times when chasing a coyote, he stopped suddenly and simply looked at me. I continued screaming, waving my hands above my head, and chasing him until he finally ran away. I was once chasing two coyotes when they suddenly turned and started running back toward me. I followed their lead by running toward them and continuing to chase them until they turned and ran. Another time, I watched a coyote jump out of a storm drain on Ellis Avenue into the channel water, then wade to an island in the channel. Several times, I watched coyotes run along the banks of the channel to a bridge, down its concrete sides, and then through the water under the bridge to the other side. On only two occasions were coyotes seen crossing a city street to enter the channel.

I once watched two coyotes trying to capture squirrels that were scampering along a block wall above them. A few times I even found coyotes sleeping on the channel floor on top of shrubs. Once I found a coyote curled up in a ball, sleeping in the dirt on the bank of the channel. Many times, a coyote would come out of nowhere, suddenly appearing right in front of me!

The coyote's scientific name is *Canis latrans*, a species of the Canidae family. The coyote is a medium-sized member of this family that also includes wolves and foxes. Coyotes have a highly organized social system consisting of packs of coyotes that defend territories from other coyotes. Packs are usually composed of an alpha male–alpha female pair along with a few other members. The alphas are usually first in command and the mating pair. Sometimes a pack will include beta adults; they are second in command to alphas, but rarely breed.

Genetic analysis has revealed that nearly all coyote pack mates are close relatives except for the alpha pair. Coyotes are primarily monogamous, which in zoological terms means having only one mate. More specifically, a mating pair may stay together for years, but may later choose new mates even though both remain alive.[29]

The paw prints of coyotes resemble those of dogs, but coyote paw prints are smaller at two-and-a-half inches long. The paw prints of both animals have four pads where the claws extend. The shape of a coyote's front paw print is different from that of a dog's, with the coyote's being more elongated and the dog's more rounded. Coyotes have a center lobe on their bottom pad that domestic dogs do not have. I show people the difference between a coyote's and a dog's front paw print by extending my hand to create the coyote's elongated paw shape and making a fist to create the dog's paw print. Finally, coyotes always travel in a straight line, whereas dogs meander more.

Coyotes can be found generally in North America and Central America, where the United States Forest Service has recognized 19 different subspecies. Only 16 of these subspecies exist in Mexico, the United States, and Canada: Mexican, San Pedro Martir, Southeastern, Durango, Northern, Tiburon Island, Plains, Mountain, Mearns, Lower Rio Grande, California valley, Peninsula, Texas plains, Northeastern, Northwest coast, and Colima.[30]

When we think of coyotes, many of us visualize the Disney cartoon versions of the animal: cute, lovable, and even entertaining. Although coyotes are normally timid and avoid people, one should remember that coyotes are wild, unpredictable, and dangerous animals. I do not haze coyotes in the evening, as I want to see what is coming in my direction so I can protect myself. One must always be alert to their surroundings when outdoors, because coyotes can appear anywhere, anytime. Because coyotes are unpredictable, it is important to always be on guard if one is encountered. After all, who wants to go through a series of painful rabies shots because of a bite or scratch by a coyote?

Because coyotes are wild, unpredictable, and dangerous animals, domestic dogs should never be allowed to play with them. I watched a video a man took of his dog playing with a coyote and my jaw dropped. The coyote was small and the dog was an 80-pound Labrador retriever, so the owner believed that he and his dog were safe due to the coyote's size. Luckily, nothing happened to the owner and dog, but things could have gone horribly wrong in a heartbeat.

One of the first stories we received from Central Park in Huntington Beach was of a dog playing with a coyote. When the coyote ran into the bushes, the dog followed, and it was attacked by the three other coyotes hiding there.

First of all, it is important to remember that when you see one coyote, it is likely that another coyote is hiding nearby, and one should always assume that is the case. Being prepared and safe is always better than the alternative. Secondly, people should never allow their dogs to play with coyotes, as this can lead to grave consequences. Finally, one should leave the area immediately if a coyote is encountered while walking a dog.

Unfortunately, once a coyote bites or scratches a person, it must be euthanized in order to test it for rabies. To reduce the risk of contracting rabies, one should avoid wild animals acting tame and tame animals acting wild (animals exhibiting any changes in normal behavior). Although wild animals contract the disease most often, domestic pets can also contract it. If you think you have been exposed to the rabies virus through the bite, scratch, or saliva of a possibly infected animal, immediately wash the affected area with plenty of soap and water. Then be sure to get medical attention and report the incident to authorities. Symptoms of rabies in people include aggressive behavior, depression, loss of appetite, and difficulty eating, drinking, and swallowing.

Between July 6 and August 1, 2015, I hazed and chased coyotes nine times in the channel behind my complex. Sometimes I found a pair of coyotes and other times found just one. By this time, I knew that my plan to haze the coyotes out of the channel within a couple weeks was unrealistic. The coyotes returned 1 to 6 days after each hazing. I continued to report my chases to the FVPD each time, because I had given the board of directors my word that I would.

On August 12, 2015, a new coyote management plan was rolled out in Long Beach in response to the growing coyote problem and the safety concerns of residents. It was a threat-level-tiered four-color response plan that identified coyote behaviors and the appropriate actions to take based on those behaviors. In first-level blue, a coyote is seen in an area and residents are expected to haze it. In second-level yellow, coyotes show no fear of people, and a more aggressive level of hazing is recommended, conducted by either residents or a newly formed volunteer hazing team. In third-level orange, a coyote is involved in an event with an attendant domestic pet animal loss; additional, more-aggressive hazing is required, including the possible removal of the coyote if multiple incidents have occurred. In the fourth level, a coyote is involved in an unprovoked encounter or attack on a human, and city staff may work to lethally remove it.

My main concern with the new coyote management plan was that it relied too heavily on residents hazing coyotes without providing instructions or training on how to do so. Also, I do not believe that one hazing team is enough for each city—a designated hazing team should be established for each neighborhood. Based on our prior attempts to encourage people to haze coyotes, we knew that most people were reluctant to haze because they were afraid of coyotes, did not want to get involved, were too busy, or were not physically capable of hazing.

People are more likely to take a picture or shoot a video of a coyote and post it on social media than they are to haze it. To establish only one hazing team for a city is not effective, because by the time the hazing team arrives at the sighting location, the coyote is long gone. My recommendation is to establish a hazing team in each neighborhood. If a coyote appears in the neighborhood, the hazing team can quickly mobilize to haze the coyote before it has a chance to leave.

By the end of August, I began to see progress with my own hazing, as I was no longer seeing pairs of coyotes in the channel. I only hazed six times in August, and each time it was of a single coyote, compared with ten hazings of one and two coyotes during July. The lower number of hazed coyotes was an improvement, but even more notable was the reduced number of sightings in August, a positive sign considering that August is the most active month for coyotes. I was also grateful that I had found no coyote pups in the channel during the time I had been hazing. I remember one time when I was chasing a coyote and he stopped to dump some scat right in front of me. I thought this was very strange until a hunter told me that wild animals will often defecate to lighten their load so that they can run faster.

On September 17, 2015, the city of Irvine decided to haze coyotes with paint guns instead of trapping and euthanizing them. So from 5:00 to 9:00 each evening, three Irvine animal services officers armed with paintball guns patrolled the Portola Springs and Pavilion Park neighborhoods to deter the animals from engaging in human contact. Their objective was to discourage coyotes from entering residential areas. The guns shot bright yellow paintball markers that stung the animals but did not cause permanent damage. If officers spotted a coyote while on patrol, they could scare it away using other means or choose to shoot, but the goal was to do so humanely.

That same day, the Live Tracker at Coyotes OC was cyberattacked using DDoS (distributed denial of service), in which large volumes of traffic are sent to a target in order to overwhelm its resources. The attack was so destructive that it took down our entire website and sent out spam to all our users. The hackers nearly destroyed the site that Carolyn Graf Matthews had worked so hard to build. We knew that the level of security on our website was not sufficient to stop the hackers, and that we would thus be forced to increase it. Unfortunately, that also meant more money. Carolyn managed to find a more secure server and decided to give it a try.

A year had passed since our last meeting at the Landmark community in Huntington Beach, so I was excited to attend the 2015 meeting to find out what had happened since 2014. When I arrived, a number of people were already seated, including HBPD Chief Robert Handy and CDFW Lt. Kent Smirl. The information they shared at the meeting was surprising, to say the least. Since the time we had last met in 2014, 150 sightings had been reported compared with just 18 in 2014. The sightings involved both single coyotes and those traveling in packs. Yet people in the audience that evening included those who admitted they had not reported sightings to HBPD. During the walk-through in Landmark after the 2014 meeting, we encountered pet food dishes outside resident units and observed landscaping that provided adequate hiding places for coyotes.

The pet food dishes were removed, and bushes were trimmed so that coyotes could not hide behind them. The Critter Busters extermination company was hired, and two coyotes were caught and euthanized within 3 weeks using beef jerky for bait. Critter Busters was the same company that Seal Beach had hired, and we were advised that more pets than coyotes had been caught during the 2 months that Critter Busters trapped there. Now residents of Landmark were expected to form a hazing team to keep coyotes out, and the panel of speakers asked for volunteers who would be trained to haze coyotes. Lt. Kent Smirl advised us that any hazing plan residents implemented would take approximately two years to be effective at driving off coyotes. Tips were also provided for keeping coyotes from homes. One Landmark resident confided to me that the coyote problem was much better now than it had been in 2014, but even so there were still coyotes at Landmark.

On September 19, 2015, another coyote attacked a small child, but this time in Los Angeles. A three-year-old girl was bitten in the neck by a coyote while playing at a playground in Elysian Park near Dodger Stadium. Coyote problems had been ongoing at Elysian Park for more than a year before four coyotes burst from the bushes that day; three ran off, and the fourth stayed behind and bit the girl. In fact, a coyote attack in Elysian Park the month before had never made the news, and city officials never provided warnings to residents. As a result, people who visited Elysian Park were unaware of the dangers and unprepared for a possible coyote encounter. Officials managed to get the coyote's DNA from the girl's body, and trappers set out to search for the animal. Two coyotes were trapped and euthanized, only for officials to find later that neither was the offender they were looking for.[31]

On October 1, 2015, I returned to the channel after work and found that the pair of coyotes had returned. It was so dark that I could barely see them, but I chased them nonetheless. I cannot tell you how frightening it was to be out in the channel, which looked to me like a large black abyss. I managed to chase those two coyotes down the channel, but it was not an easy task. Because I had seen only one coyote in the month before, I hoped this would be the last time I saw coyotes in October.

During this time, Long Beach residents retained the law firm Michel and Associates, P.C., and sent a letter asking city officials to take control of the aggressive urban coyotes in their city for public safety reasons. The author of the letter was well informed on the subject of coyotes and cited prior research by Rex Baker, PhD at California State Polytechnic University, Pomona, California, as evidence that hazing alone was not enough to address the coyote problem. Some misleading rumors surrounding coyotes that were being presented to the general public were addressed and debunked. The author also pointed out prior successful coyote management programs that utilized the removal of coyotes in order to instill fear of humans in the remaining coyotes and reduce their habituation. According to the author, the letter to Long Beach city officials was merely a warning that residents were quite concerned about their safety and the safety of their pets.

Unfortunately, I had not seen the last of the coyotes in the channel, because 2 days later I saw a single coyote, and the following day I saw a pair. The coyotes were testing me again! So where had they been for the past month, and why had they returned? Then it occurred to me that this was the new group of juveniles who were looking for new home ranges and territories. Once again, I chased the coyotes and reported my sightings to the FVPD.

Several days passed with no coyotes being seen in the channel. It was getting dark earlier in the evening, and I knew that I could not continue to chase coyotes every night. Soon I would be driving to and from work in the dark. I considered not chasing coyotes daily, instead limiting my chasing to weekends only so that I could chase during daylight hours. Let me tell you, it is a frightening experience to walk a channel at night, alone, throwing rocks down to the channel floor but without being able to see a thing.

On the evening of October 15, 2015, a fourth coyote attacked a small child and his father in Irvine. Just after six o'clock, the father was working in the garage, and his three-year-old son was playing in the yard, when a coyote bit the child on the right knee. The child ran to his father, who was bent over, and jumped onto his father's back. The father thought his son was playing until the coyote bit the father's buttocks. Both father and son were treated by paramedics and driven to a hospital for further medical attention. The coyote ran off before officers with the Irvine Police Department's Animal Services division arrived.[32]

By daylight savings time on November 1, 2015, I had decided to haze coyotes on weekends only. Even after the clocks were set back an hour in California, it still became dark too early in the evening for me to haze during daylight hours. I thought about all the hunting time coyotes would have now that the evenings had become longer. And I thought of all the pets that would become victims of coyote attacks during the long fall and winter nights. Needless to say, fall and winter are not my favorite times of the year.

When a neighborhood first discovers that it has a coyote problem, it can be unsettling for everyone concerned. When discussing options with such groups, I usually start by describing the hunting process, explaining that when coyotes hunt, they choose one neighborhood and conduct hunting sweeps there until they have hunted it out and can no longer find food. Coyotes may continue hunting for days, weeks, or even months in a single neighborhood, provided that they continue to find food. Once the food sources are gone, coyotes move on to the next neighborhood, again hunting until they can no longer find food. Then they move on to the next neighborhood and repeat the process.

This clever hunting technique is methodical and cyclical. They move from neighborhood to neighborhood, allowing formerly hunted neighborhoods to replenish their food sources before eventually returning to the first neighborhood to hunt it again.

Of course, feeding coyotes is not a solution but actually perpetuates the problem—coyotes not only move on to another neighborhood when they can no longer find food in their existing one, but they will not leave a neighborhood if food is being provided to them.

The best way to avoid feeding coyotes inadvertently is by keeping all food and pets indoors where coyotes cannot get to them, and by reducing pet odor with white vinegar or ammonia applied to patios, sidewalks, and driveways. If scat (compost) is found, one should use rubber gloves for removal and dispose of the scat immediately. It does not matter whether it is dog scat or coyote scat. Dog scat attracts coyotes. Coyotes mark homes that contain potential prey (your pets) by leaving scat in the yard, on the driveway, or on the sidewalk near the home, so scat that is not removed becomes a hunting marker when they return.

Female coyotes are more likely to mark territories with urine than with scat; they simply squat and urinate. If a female coyote urinates on your grass, the good news is that the odor is reduced each time the grass is watered, making it more difficult for the female coyote to find her marked spot. Coyotes have a heightened sense of smell and can smell pet odor, including compost odors that you cannot smell, so all pet compost should be kept in an airtight container until disposal.

Along the same lines, one should keep trash in airtight, sealable, animal-proof containers. Coyotes love trash and will make an easy meal of leftovers if they can open the trash can. Coyotes also love fruit, and fruit scents attract them, so one should be sure to pick up fallen fruit and remove ripe fruit from trees. Bird feeders should also be removed, as bird feeders attract mice and birds, which in turn attract coyotes.

On November 4, 2015, we learned that the coyote responsible for three of the five biting incidents in Irvine's Portola Springs had been trapped and euthanized.[33] By this time, a total of ten coyotes had been euthanized, but only two had been linked to the attacks through DNA. Although trapping and euthanizing efforts by officials may have seemed unsuccessful at first glance, they helped make coyotes fearful of people again. This success is indicated by the absence of new stories of coyote attacks or sightings from the Portola

Springs neighborhood following the euthanization of the tenth coyote. Authorities finally caught the main culprit. Two Portola Springs attacks might have been prevented if the open garage door in each case had instead been closed.

Increased coyote sightings and attacks in Newport Beach, California, prompted a November 4, 2015 meeting. More than 80 people attended the Speak Up Newport meeting at the Civic Center Community Room. The meeting did not go as planned, as residents started demanding that something be done about the coyote problem and began yelling at officials. Michelle Steel, a member of the Orange County Board of Supervisors, was present to discuss a new policy for all Orange County cities to follow.[34]

9

THE COYOTE MANAGEMENT PLAN

November 8, 2015, was the last time I saw coyotes in the channel that year. It was a pair, and I chased them all the way down the channel, under the Brookhurst Street bridge, and toward Garfield. In October, I had chased single coyotes and pairs six different times. In total, over a span of less than 5 months, I had chased coyotes and called the FVPD to report my sightings 26 times. It was hard to believe that I had finally accomplished what I had set out to do—persuade coyotes to leave from the channel behind my complex. I admit that for several weeks after, I kept expecting to see a coyote jump out of the bushes every time I returned to the channel, but I never did.

It was during this time that we began receiving reports of coyotes on both residential and main streets, cutting across streets and dodging traffic. Our main concern was public safety. We were afraid that some-one might swerve to avoid hitting a coyote and instead cause an automobile accident and possibly injure others. On November 11, 2015, a picture was taken of a coyote running southbound in the number 3 lane of northbound Beach Boulevard at Garfield Avenue in Huntington Beach, California, during early morning rush hour traffic. Beach Boulevard is one of the busiest streets in Huntington Beach, and it is amazing that this coyote was not hit by a car and did not cause an accident that morning.

A Huntington Beach, California, town hall meeting was held on November 23, 2015 at the First Christian Church on Main Street. In attendance were city councilmembers, representatives from CDFW, Police Chief Robert Handy, Dan Fox of Animal Pest Management Services, residents, pro-coyote removal activists, animal rights activists, and a member of the Orange County Board of Supervisors—Michelle Steel. Michelle Steel began the meeting with a discussion about how cities in Orange County were handling the coyote problem, as each one was handling it differently, and indicated that she would like to see more consistency, with all cities adopting similar plans. Residents lined up to share their stories with the panel—mostly coyote attacks on pets—and to voice concerns about the growing lack of fear of people shown by coyotes and the ensuing public safety threat.

Chief Robert Handy indicated that from January to November, 470 coyote sightings and 78 coyote attacks on animals were reported. Huntington Beach officials were trying to find a solution to the growing coyote problem. Animal rights activists did not agree with the trapping plan proposal, stating that trapping does not work. As discussion came to a close, officials appeared to be leaning toward a plan to approve the trapping of one to four coyotes. The town hall meeting came to a close outside with a Native American song and dance performance.

To illustrate the importance of keeping doors closed at all times, that same evening a coyote entered a Laguna Beach bedroom and snatched a Chihuahua, Eloise, through the open door of a bedroom where a three-week-old baby was sleeping. When John Fischer heard his three dogs barking, he assumed that a guest he was expecting had arrived. John did not panic until he saw a coyote running out of the bedroom with eight-year-old Eloise in its jaws. Because coyotes look for movement when they hunt, the coyote's attention had been drawn to the dogs in the bedroom rather than the baby. Although Fischer lost his beloved Eloise that day, he and his family had much to be grateful for— his granddaughter was not disturbed while she slept, and the dogs were in the bedroom and thus diverted the coyote's attention from his granddaughter.[35]

The following day, a friend asked me if I had seen the new coyote management plan for Newport Beach and sent me the link. As I read the plan, I realized that it was quite similar to the one in Long Beach. Both plans proposed a tiered four-color threat-level matrix that identified coyote behaviors and the appropriate actions to take based on those behaviors. In the final draft of the Long Beach coyote management plan, first-level green was replaced with blue. Long Beach officials believed that green signified an inappropriate "go" message to residents, so they decided that blue was more suitable. Although the two plans were similar, each was modified to fit its city's individual needs. The new coyote management plan also resembled a four-color plan being implemented in Canada. The coyote management plan was designed to be generic enough for both rural and urban community use. Similar coyote management plans have been adopted in Denver, Colorado; Riverside, Illinois; and New Castle, New York; and the list of cities continues to grow daily.

Although the author of the plan was never disclosed, it did not take long to find the same coyote management plan information on the HSUS website. Many people do not know that HSUS is part of a large international organization. In Canada, Central America, Europe, and Australia, it operates under the name Humane Society International. HSUS was designed to manage political lobbying for animal welfare so that smaller state fish and game agencies and local animal shelters with limited funding and staff would not be burdened with this task. A large part of the money used in political lobbying funds by HSUS is generated through public donations.

When city officials adopt a new coyote management plan, it is important that the public welfare is safeguarded. As with any plan to deter coyotes, a coyote management plan must incorporate a multi-pronged approach that gives officials several options. Coyotes have different personalities and therefore may respond differently to similar circumstances. Each year coyotes are becoming more habituated, so actions that may have worked to deter coyotes one year may not be effective in the next. The ideal coyote management plan will incorporate several different options, and will reserve lethal management as a last resort. Because it is unknown how long the coyote population will continue increasing and how habituated they will become during that time, any coyote plan adopted by a city should not be limited in its options.

The goal of the plan is to support coexistence with urban coyotes using education, behavior modification, and development of a tiered response to aggressive coyote behavior. To reach this goal, the city develops three primary strategies: public education, enforcement of laws and regulations prohibiting the feeding of wildlife, and appropriate tiered responses to coyote–human interactions. These strategies require active participation on the part of the entire community. However, we had not been provided information on what exactly community participation would be and whether any training would be provided to the community.

The following is a brief overview of the plan. Simply insert the name of your city every time you see the word "city," and you can see that this plan was designed to be easily implemented in any city in North America.

Management Strategy

City strategy for managing coyotes is based on balancing respect and protection for wildlife and their habitats without compromising public safety. The main strategy comprises a three-pronged approach:

1. Public education should be designed around coexistence with coyotes.

2. Laws and regulations prohibiting the feeding of wildlife should be enforced.

3. Ensuring public safety by implementing appropriate tiered responses to coyote and human interactions. This plan requires active participation on the part of the entire community including residents, HOAs, volunteers, and city personnel. Education is the key to having residents make appropriate decisions regarding their safety or managing their property and pets.

Coyote Management Plan—Background

The city does not own or have control of wild animals found within its boundaries, nor is the city responsible for the actions or damage caused by them. These animals are a common and important integral part of our ecosystem. City animal control officers typically do not respond to calls for service for normal coyote events such as sightings. However, they will respond to calls that involve a sick or injured coyote or constitute a public safety issue, such as a coyote threatening people or resting in an area frequented by people, such as a yard, park, playground, or school.

Difficulties Managing Wildlife

Although the city places a high value on its wildlife, some individual animals adapted to urban environments have the potential to cause problems and/or conflicts in specific situations. In addressing problems, the city promotes policies supporting prevention and implementation of remedial measures that do not harm wildlife or their habitats.

A wildlife problem is defined as any situation that causes a health or safety issue to its residents.

Relocation of animals is not ecologically sound, as relocated animals generally do not survive the transfer. If they do, they rarely stay in the relocation area and tend to disperse to other locations where they may cause problems to humans, be involved in territorial disputes or introduce disease. In some instances, the translocated coyote will go to great lengths to return to its previous territory. As a last resort, lethal control measures, when employed, are controversial and nonselective, meaning they target the alpha coyote or problem coyote. If they are used, they must be humane and in compliance with federal and state laws.

It is not economically, ecologically, or in other ways justified to attempt to remove all coyotes from the urban ecosystem as a means of addressing conflicts between humans and coyotes. Attempts have been made to eradicate coyotes over the past century by local, state, and federal agencies, as well as private organizations, but have been proven ineffective. Moreover, during the past century coyotes have expanded their territories to include every state except Hawaii.

What Role Does the Coyote Play in the Environment?

Coyotes play an important role in the urban ecosystem, particularly as a top predator. They eat a broad range of small animals, including squirrels, mice, rabbits, rats and gophers. Rodents make up a majority of their diet. In the process, they control the population sizes of these animals, many of which are considered pests to humans. Coyotes also prey on "mesopredators" such as raccoons and opossums. Without a top predator like the coyote to keep them in check, meso-predators can dramatically reduce bird populations by eating their eggs. Coyotes also disperse seeds of native plant species and recycle nutrients. In general, coyotes regularly roam an area of about two to five square miles to obtain enough food for the pack members. Normally, each pack is a territorial family group made up of three to ten individuals. A portion of the area the pack inhabits is the pack's territory, which they will defend from other coyotes. The number of mature coyotes in the pack is often related to the amount of food resources in the territory.

A coyote pack usually has only one breeding (or alpha) female. This female often produces more pups than can be supported by the pack. Young coyotes may leave the pack at about 9 to 11 months of age, but dispersal patterns are highly variable. These juvenile coyotes become transients. Other types of transients include older individuals that can no longer defend their role as upper-level pack members and are pushed out of the pack.

Transients move all over in narrow undefended zones that exist between pack territories searching for an open habitat to occupy or group to join. They often die before they succeed (many are hit by cars). It is largely because of the constant influx of transients that coyote eradication programs fail.

Monitoring and Collecting Data

Monitoring and data collection are critical components of an effective coyote management plan. This is best accomplished with input from both residents and city officials. Coyote sightings or incidents can be made by calling the local city Police Department or Animal Control Services. The purpose of monitoring human–coyote interactions is to document where coyotes are frequently seen and identify human–coyote conflict hot spots if they exist. Gathering specific data on incidents will allow for targeting of educational campaigns and conflict mitigation efforts, as well as the ability to measure success in reducing conflicts over time.

Public Education and Outreach

Education is the key to having residents make appropriate decisions regarding their safety or managing their property and pets. This involves decreasing attractants, increasing pet safety and creating reasonable expectations of normal coyote behavior.

Learning how to respond to a coyote encounter empowers residents and can help reduce undesired coyote behaviors. The public should understand what normal coyote behavior is when living in close proximity with coyotes. For example, vocalization is normal acceptable behavior and does not indicate aggression. Education and outreach efforts by the city should focus on:

- understanding human safety, pet safety, coyote attractants, deterrents to coyotes on private property, including appropriate fencing, exclusion techniques, "what to do" tips, and information on appropriate hazing techniques

- developing a common language and awareness of normal versus abnormal behavior when discussing encounters with coyotes

- disseminating information to residents, businesses and schools through the city's website, social media, traditional media, fliers/handouts, mailers, etc.

- consulting with land managers, nonprofit organizations like the HSUS and agencies like the state Department of Fish and Game that provide public education materials, programs and expertise

Coyote Attractants in Urban Areas

Coyotes are drawn to urban and suburban areas for the following reasons:

1. **Food**. Urban areas often support large numbers of rodents. However, coyotes can be further attracted into suburban neighborhoods by human-associated food such as pet food, unsecured compost or trash and fallen fruit in yards. Intentional and unintentional feeding can lead coyotes to associate

humans with sources of food, which can result in negative interactions among coyotes, people, and pets. To reduce food attractants in urban and suburban areas:

a. Never hand-feed or otherwise deliberately feed a coyote.

b. Avoid feeding pets outside. Remove sources of pet food and water that a coyote could easily obtain. If feeding pets outside is necessary, remove the bowl and leftover food promptly.

c. Never include meat or dairy in compost.

d. Maintain good housekeeping, such as regularly raking areas around bird feeders.

e. Remove fallen fruit from the ground.

f. Keep trash in high-quality containers with tight-fitting lids. Only place the cans curbside the morning of collection. If you leave out overnight, trash cans are more likely to be tipped over and explored.

g. Bag especially attractive food wastes, such as meat scraps or leftover pet food, before discarding.

2. **Water.** Urban areas provide a year-round supply of water in the form of storm water impoundments and channels, artificial lakes, irrigation, pet water dishes, etc., that support both coyotes and their prey. During drought and other dry conditions, water can be as alluring as food, so remove water bowls set outside for pets and make watering cans unavailable.

3. **Access to shelter.** Parks, greenbelts, open spaces, golf courses, buildings, sheds, decks and crawl spaces, etc., increase the amount and variability of cover for coyotes.

   In the spring, when coyotes give birth and begin to raise their young, they concentrate their activities around dens or burrows in which their young are sheltered. Coyotes may also use spaces under sheds or decks for use as a den.

4. **Unattended Pets.** Pets are a normal part of an urban landscape. Within their territory, coyotes may consider pets potential prey or potential competitors.

   a. Free-roaming pets, especially cats and sometimes small dogs, may attract coyotes into neighborhoods. The best way to minimize risk to pets is to not leave them outside unattended.

   b. Cats. Coyotes primarily eat small mammals such as mice, but will also prey on slightly larger mammals such as rabbits. Approximately the same size as a rabbit, free-roaming outdoor cats may also be seen as prey by coyotes.

   c. Feral cats. People who feed feral cats are often concerned that coyotes might prey on the cats. These concerns are well founded, as coyotes can be attracted to the outdoor pet food. Although there is no sure way to protect feral cats from coyotes, the following tips can be helpful:

      i. Do not feed feral cats. Doing so can have unintentional consequences, including ecological damage.

      ii. Provide escape routes for cats.

     iii. Haze coyotes seen on the property. Making them feel uncomfortable will encourage them to stay out of the area.

   d. Dogs are also vulnerable to coyote confrontations:

      i. Small, unattended dogs may be seen by coyotes as prey.

     ii. Although attacks on larger dogs are rarer, coyotes will sometimes go after a large dog when they feel that their territory is threatened. This generally occurs during the coyote breeding season.

     iii. Do not allow dogs off leash, off your property.

Hazing and Behavioral Change

Some coyotes have become too comfortable in the close proximity of people. For coyotes to safely coexist with people, they must fear and avoid contact with humans.

Hazing—also known as "fear conditioning"—is the process that facilitates this change in coyote behavior and is by necessity a community response to negative encounters with coyotes. The more often an individual animal is hazed, the more effective hazing is in changing coyote behavior.

Goals of Hazing

1. Reshape coyote behavior to avoid human contact in an urban setting.

2. Give residents tools to actively engage in reshaping coyote behavior and to support feeling safe in their parks and neighborhoods.

3. Model appropriate and effective hazing behavior.

Overview of Hazing

Hazing must continue once it begins until the animal leaves. Otherwise, the coyote will learn to "wait" until the person gives up. Not following through with hazing will create an animal more resistant to hazing.

Hazing never involves injury to the animal, only the threat of injury. An injured animal becomes less predictable.

A common concern with hazing involves potential danger to the hazer. A coyote's basic nature is very skittish and this nature is what makes the technique useful. A normal, healthy coyote is very unlikely to escalate a situation with a person who is aggressively hazing. It is important that the hazer provides the coyote a clear escape route to flee and not corner the animal.

The following are elements of an effective hazing campaign:

1. Pet owners should protect their pets. Off-leash and unattended dogs and unattended outside cats attract coyotes (as does pet food).
2. Residents should learn hazing effectiveness and techniques. A hazing program must be instituted, maintained and evaluated on a regular basis.
3. Hazing needs to be active for a sustained period to achieve the desired change in behavior.
4. Hazing requires monitoring to assess its effectiveness and to determine if further action or more aggressive hazing is needed.

Response Plan

A detailed tiered response plan has been developed to provide a mechanism for identifying and classifying different levels of human and coyote interactions.

Threat-Level Tiered Response

Level Green—Behavior: A coyote is seen or heard in an area. Sighting may be during the day or night. Coyote may be seen moving through the area. Response: Education and hazing needed.

Level Yellow—Behavior: A coyote appears to frequently associate with humans or human-related food sources, and exhibits little wariness of human presence. Coyote is seen during the day resting or continuously moving through an area frequented by people. Response: Education and aggressive hazing needed, volunteer hazing team created.

Level Orange—Behavior: A coyote is involved in an incident with an attendant domestic animal loss. Several level-orange incidents in the same general area may indicate the presence of a habituated coyote(s). Response: Education and aggressive hazing needed, volunteer hazing team created, and public awareness of incident(s) and circumstances discussed. If multiple level-orange incidents have occurred in the same vicinity within a short amount of time, lethal removal may be recommended.

Level Red—Behavior: A coyote that has been involved in an investigated and documented provoked or unprovoked close encounter or attack on humans. Response: city staff may work to lethally remove the responsible coyote(s) after a thorough investigation of the incident(s).

Once again, my main concern with the new coyote management plan is that it relies too heavily on residents hazing coyotes without providing sufficient instructions or training on how to do so, as discussed in greater detail in the immediately preceding chapter.

In 2014, we saw a coyote go through Jim Geissinger's closed screen door in Laguna Woods, California, and snatch his cat Cheeto out of the sunroom. However, we never expected to see a coyote jump through a glass window, snapping at a man at a Greyhound bus terminal in Dallas, Texas, on December 1, 2015. The bus terminal was evacuated and the coyote was chased out of the bus terminal by two security officers and policemen. Anytime a coyote exhibits unusual behavior, the coyote is believed to be sick. The coyote was released, so it is unknown why the coyote jumped through the glass window that day, but the incident showed us that coyotes were capable of going through glass, too.[36]

On December 2, 2015, the Coyotes OC Live Tracker was taken down in another DDoS attack. This time the attack was so destructive that Carolyn Graf Matthews and I were at a crossroads. We had worked hard to build the database, create informational material to help educate people about coyotes, and had successfully increased awareness of coyote activity in neighborhoods, just to have our database destroyed by hackers! Now to continue on, we had to rebuild the website and find an even more secure server for our database, which would cost even more money. We thought it over for a couple weeks and decided to start collecting donations for a new, more secure server, because many people still were not aware of coyotes in their neighborhoods. By this time, we had collected more than 830 reports of coyote sightings and attacks and had added Riverside, Los Angeles, and San Diego Counties to our Live Tracker.

Between 250,000 and 750,000 coyotes live in California, the majority in densely populated cities. During 2015, 24 coyote bites were reported in those densely populated areas. Fourteen people were bitten in Los Angeles County, with nine occurring near Dodger Stadium at Elysian Park. Perhaps if more media attention had been given to the coyote attacks in Elysian Park, some of those attacks could have been prevented.

The reason coyotes are drawn to more densely populated areas is because of the greater availability of food. People intentionally and unintentionally feed coyotes with their pet food, trash, fruit, and sometimes even pets or livestock left outside unattended. As a result, coyotes thrive in densely populated areas, and urban coyotes are bigger, healthier, live longer, and have larger litters, so it is no surprise that the urban coyote population continues to grow.

My neighborhood used to be a cat community, but it no longer is. Only one of the seven cats (Orange) that were trapped and treated remains in our neighborhood today. In fact, cats are rarely seen any more on the greenbelts, whereas several once lounged there during the day. Some families have lost one, two, and even three cats, presumably to coyotes. And although coyotes no longer live in the channel behind my community, we know that they pass through in the evenings, as evidenced by the scat and tracks left behind.

When we walk along the Santa Ana River now, we rarely see wildlife other than the occasional rabbit, mouse, rat, gopher, lizard, crow, hawk, or seagull. We never see squirrels, skunks, ducks, and weasels like we used to, and we wonder if they will ever return. The one fox seen by a Huntington Beach resident last May has not been seen since. The yards of homes along the river are riddled with gopher holes, and residents continue to find rats and mice inside their homes. Exterminators still make a lucrative living removing gophers, mice, and rats from those homes.

Probably the most gruesome story ever shared with Coyotes OC was one that unfolded on December 16, 2015, when a neighbor decided to check on Terence Griffin, Jr., an elderly, retired, single man who had not been seen for some time. The neighbor called Griffin's maid, who told her that she had not seen Griffin for approximately three months, but that she still had his house key. The neighbor met the maid that day at the Long Beach, California, home. The two women experienced difficulty opening the door, because mail had piled up behind it.

A second neighbor joined them after they had managed to get the door open, and all three walked inside and into the den. The sliding glass door to the backyard was wide open, even though Griffin's dog had passed away 6 months before.

It looked as if a fire had occurred, based on the brown spot that the neighbor observed on the sofa. Skeletal remains and a human skull could be seen in the center of the room, and more bones were scattered throughout. The three got out of the house and called 911.

Long Beach Fire and Police personnel responded. The Los Angeles County Coroner's report indicated that the skeletonized remains found at the residence possibly resulted from dismemberment by animals.

Several bones were missing, and the cause of death could not be determined from the eight-and-a-half pounds of bones collected. (A human body has a minimum of 15 pounds of bone.) The bones had been picked clean.

One officer told the coroner investigator that police believed the decedent had died in his residence, and the remains were damaged because the resident had not locked down or secured his home. The officer also commented that the area was known by police to have a heavy coyote population.[37]

Further review of the coroner's report, which
lacked detail, indicates that Griffin passed away
approximately one month before his remains were
found. Cause of death could not be determined by the
county coroner based on the remains collected. Of the
feces scattered on the floor of the home, only rat and
bird waste were identified, although it seems likely
that raccoons, rats, and coyotes were present as well.

Prior reports had been made of coyotes entering homes in nearby Leisure World to hunt for food,
so it was not uncommon for coyotes to enter homes
in that area. Based on prior coyote reports from residents in Long Beach, significant coyote activity had
occurred in Griffin's neighborhood prior to his death.
Unfortunately, the Long Beach Police Department
never contacted CDFW in order to enlist its expertise in identifying the feces that had been scattered
throughout the house, so we will never know with
certainty what other scavengers may have been inside
Griffin's home.

10

CONCLUSION

Perhaps there was a reason why my cat Big Boy was attacked, killed, and eaten by a coyote back in 2011. After all, if Big Boy's attack had never happened, I would not be sharing my story with you today. At some point the coyote population can be expected to drop back down to reasonable levels. Even so, coyotes will always be here. We must remain cautious and continue to protect our small children and pets from coyotes at all times, even when the threat may seem to have lessened.

As coyotes become more habituated, they also become more visible to people. As a result, a reduction in the coyote population may not be visibly evident, as reduced numbers will be offset by increased visibility. But I believe we will see indicators of coyotes succumbing to disease. If the disease is mange, we will see a greater number of coyotes losing fur in the earlier stages, and with pink spots or lesions that have lost their fur almost completely (chupacabras) in the final stages. If the disease is something other than mange, we will begin seeing a greater number of very skinny and sickly looking coyotes. Regardless of the disease, one should always stay away from sick coyotes, as they are quite unpredictable and dangerous.

In the meantime, the only way that we can affect coyote habituation is by hazing them every time we see them. If coyotes are hazed every time they encounter people, they will learn to associate unpleasant experiences with people and will stay away if the unpleasantry continues and is reinforced. The more that coyotes are hazed, the less habituated they become, and this should result in fewer human and coyote conflicts.

Every time a person sees a coyote and takes no action, the coyote is being taught that people are nothing to fear, and habituation increases. Eventually, a habituated coyote will become so brazen that it is identified as a nuisance coyote and a threat to humans. Habituated coyotes are eventually removed (usually by euthanization), so please save a coyote—instead of taking a picture or videotaping a coyote when you see it, haze it to keep it fearful of humans.

Coyote Preparedness References

R1. *Coyotes can adapt to almost any environment in their search for food and shelter. They can and will:*

- squeeze through a 3"–4" gap in a fence or wall
- leap over a 4' fence or wall without touching it
- jump over a 5'–7' fence or wall by first jumping from the ground to the top of the barrier, then to the ground on the other side
- utilize foliage (vine plants, bushes, trees) to manipulate themselves to the top of walls up to 8' high
- slide under a chain link fence through a very small clearance
- dig a tunnel under a fence in a matter of minutes
- travel alongside fences, walls, bushes, and buildings, where it is more difficult to see them
- travel as fast as 40 mph
- use their heightened senses to smell, see, and hear things humans cannot

R2. *Tips to make your home less attractive to coyotes:*

- Coyotes have a heightened sense of smell, so attempt to eliminate and reduce odors around your home.
- Pour ammonia or white vinegar on your patio and in your yard.

- If you have a dog, be sure to pick up after it, as its compost will attract coyotes.
- Never leave food or water outside.
- Always clean up after a barbecue.
- Pick fruit from trees and from the ground if any has fallen there.
- Keep trash cans covered and inside your garage, as coyotes are attracted to the odors of trash.
- Alternate the turn-on times of your sprinkler system weekly, or install motion-activated sprinklers. Changing the sprinkler turn-on time prevents coyotes from developing a habit of visiting your home at a certain time each day.
- Cut back low-lying bushes so that coyotes cannot hide behind them.
- Increase outdoor lighting and install motion detectors.
- Purchase wolf or bear urine (PeeMart.com has a good selection at reasonable prices) and sprinkle it in your yard once a week.
- Remove bird feeders to reduce the number of rodents that may attract coyotes.
- Buy an ultrasonic or electronic device that emits a high-frequency noise, and Nite Guard, which has a flashing red light that repels coyotes. Periodically, move these devices to different locations around your yard. Nite Guard also manufactures a repellent tape that makes noise and creates light flashes that deter predators.

R3. *Hazing methods*

Hazing is the method of using deterrents to move an animal out of an area or discourage its undesirable behavior or activity. Hazing can help maintain coyotes' fear of humans and keep them out of backyards and playgrounds. The following are some examples of hazing:

- Raise your arms, wave your hands, and shout while approaching the coyote; make yourself large and loud!
- Use noisemakers such as your voice, whistles, air horns, bells, and soda cans filled with pennies or dead batteries. If you have a pet, use your noisemaker in your home for a few weeks with your pet nearby to familiarize it with the noisemaker. Continue until your pet no longer reacts to the noise.
- Use projectiles such as sticks, small rocks, cans, tennis balls, and rubber balls. Throw these projectiles near the coyote but not directly at it.
- Use other repellents such as hoses, water guns with vinegar water, spray bottles with vinegar water, pepper spray, bear repellent, walking sticks, golf clubs, baseball bats, and pet correctors.

R4. *Things to remember while outdoors:*

Never turn your back on a coyote, and never run from one. Instead, look it straight in the eyes and scream loudly, raise your arms, and wave your hands wildly! If that does not work, throw rocks in the direction of the coyote (but not directly at it). Be alert to your surroundings at all times while outdoors. And for your protection, carry one or more of the following items with you:

- walking cane or stick
- animal Taser (stun gun)
- golf club
- baseball bat
- mace, pepper, or bear spray
- air horn
- whistle

- Super Soaker filled with water
- Pet Corrector (which uses compressed air to emit a loud hissing sound like that of a cat or snake)

It is always best to chase a coyote until he is out of sight. If you are unable to chase the coyote for any reason, however, back away slowly, looking it directly in the eyes constantly until it is out of sight.

R5. *Breaking old and bad habits*

Many of us develop risky habits without realizing that our actions could endanger our pets, such as leaving doors open so that pets can travel between the house and yard as they please, allowing our pets to be outside unattended, not picking up pet compost or fallen fruit, keeping outside trash in cans without locking lids, and hanging bird feeders in our yards.

Creating new, safe habits may seem awkward at first, but in short time you should easily adapt to a new routine. You can begin with these new safe habits:

- Store trash in covered, heavy-duty containers at all times. Use trash barrels fitted with pipe clamping devices on the lips to prevent spills. Do not put trash cans out the night before the scheduled pick up; put them out in the morning. Coyotes are intelligent and learn to knock cans over in order to access their contents.
- Keep all food indoors, including pet food.
- Pick up fallen fruit from fruit trees—particularly avocados. Fallen fruit also attracts coyote prey.
- Though coyotes generally hunt between sunset and sunrise, they can be observed at all hours of the day, so small dogs, cats, and children should not be allowed outside alone or unsupervised at any time or for any length of time, even in a fenced yard.

- Eliminate garbage, debris, and lumber piles from your house's exterior, as these could be used for shelter.
- Never allow small children to walk dogs alone.
- Change automatic sprinkler settings regularly or install motion-activated sprinklers.
- Do not feed or provide water to coyotes or other wildlife.
- Remove bird feeders from your yard.
- Pick up pet compost regularly, as it attracts coyotes, and store it in a container with a tightly fitting lid.
- Always walk your dog on a short leash (approximately six feet long), even when taking your dog outside to do its business before bedtime. This allows you to quickly pull your dog in close if a coyote appears.
- Move patio furniture around often, as this creates an unfamiliar surrounding for coyotes.
- Break the routines of letting your pet outside or walking your dogs at the same time each day, as coyotes will watch people for up to 3 weeks to learn their schedule before attempting an attack.
- Never leave doors open, and always close them behind you.
- Never open windows more than 1 or 2 inches, and secure them with locks.
- Install security screens on windows and doors.
- Remove pet doors or lock them when not in use.

R6. *Coyotes and German shepherds*

Coyotes look like German shepherds—how can one tell the difference between the two? Coyotes and German shepherds are similar in height and fur color (varying from lighter gray, white, tan, and brown mixes in desert areas to darker colors in the mountains).

Even so, coyotes are distinct from German shepherds in a few ways. They:

- have wide pointed ears and a long tapered muzzle
- have long slender legs, small feet, and a straight, bushy tail
- have a black-tipped (and sometimes white-tipped) tail
- can jump over and scale fences and block walls with relative ease
- run faster than German shepherds (40 mph versus 20–30 mph)
- have paw print tracks that are more elongated and less rounded than those of German shepherds
- are smaller than German shepherds, although their long slender legs and bushy fur make them look larger than they are; they actually weigh less than German shepherds (20–50 lbs. versus 75–95 lbs.)
- can bark like German shepherds, but also make a yipping sound that German shepherds cannot

R7. *An email sent to the Director, Humane Wildlife Conflict Resolution, HSUS, on October 23, 2014—here is how "Coyotes in Orange County, CA" came about:*

When Carolyn Matthews of Huntington Beach, California, started her blog "Coyotes in Orange County, CA" on Facebook 3 years ago, she was looking for solutions to the coyote problem.

Neighbors watched as a coyote killed Carolyn's cat in her driveway. Before this, Carolyn had had no idea that coyotes were even in her neighborhood.

Shortly thereafter, my community in Fountain Valley, California, came under coyote attack. Every week, we found cat parts in our playground, in our pool area, and at our clubhouse. We waited a year for the coyotes to leave, but they never did.

During this time, we both researched and discussed various solutions to the problem. During this process, we realized that many people were not even aware that coyotes existed in their neighborhoods.

Our first task was to attend city council meetings and ask city councils to insert flyers into water bills that warned residents about potential coyotes in their neighborhoods. We also asked city councils to hang warning signs in public parks where residents walked dogs. This helped increase awareness in our communities.

In the meantime, Carolyn and I came up with a few ideas about how to make our communities less desirable to coyotes. We implemented our ideas and created a hostile environment as we attempted to persuade the coyotes to leave (by hazing and chasing them, increasing outdoor lighting, clearing the channel of brush and debris, mending fences, cutting back bushes, pouring wolf urine in the channel, pouring ammonia and white vinegar on patios and in yards to reduce pet odors, and setting a live trap at night (we never caught anything other than a feral cat and an opossum, both of which we released). Within a short time, we stopped finding cat parts in our community, and stopped seeing coyotes altogether. Ever since, we have been helping others solve their coyote problems, and have learned the importance of education in the process. We have grown in size and are now a small group of volunteers. All of us work full time at other jobs or have other full-time responsibilities.

Our mission statement is simple:

> *To keep people, their families, and their pets safe from wildlife through information and education.*

We strive to remain unbiased when educating people about coyotes, providing only the information necessary to educate people to find effective solutions for their coyote problems.

We recently introduced a Live Coyote Tracker on our website so that anyone can pull up wild animal sightings by zip code or city and see the activity in their own neighborhood at any time. I believe our Live Tracker is the first of its kind.

Thank you for sharing an interest in Coyotes in Orange County, CA on Facebook.

I hope the information I have provided has successfully answered any questions you may have had regarding Coyotes in Orange County, CA.

R8. *Coyote life expectancy:*
- The life span of urban coyotes is 7–11 years.
- Urban coyotes in captivity can live 13–15 years.
- Coyotes have one litter per year and two to twelve pups per litter.
- Coyote pups in urban areas generally have a 60% chance of surviving their first year.
- A female coyote can have as many as 70 pups during her lifetime.
- Survival rates of juvenile coyotes in urban areas are approximately five times higher than those reported for juvenile coyotes in rural areas.

- The most common cause of death for urban coyotes is collisions with vehicles (40%–70% of deaths).
- Other causes of death include shootings, malnutrition, and disease (primarily mange).

R9. *Things you can do to coyote-proof your fence or wall:*

- Clear all vines, bushes, and trees away from the fence or block wall.
- Block gaps in the fence or wall that are more than three inches wide.
- Anchor the fence by digging and placing a chain link apron or L-footer 8 to 18 inches below the soil, so that coyotes cannot dig under your fence. (Block walls already have concrete and rebar below the surface that may deter coyotes from digging.)
- Add apron extensions (or coyote rollers if they are within your budget) to the top of the fence so that coyotes cannot climb over the fence. Some residents use bird or cat spikes on their fences to keep unwanted animals from their yards. However, bird or cat spikes have not yet been tested for effectiveness with coyotes.
- If you have a chain link fence, feed six-foot slats through the entire fence to block the coyote's line of sight into your yard (coyotes are visual hunters) and make it more difficult for it to get its footing for climbing over the fence.
- Install a 2,000- to 4,000-volt electric fence in your backyard. An electric fence can provide effective protection from a coyote. However, beyond the costs of purchasing and installing an electric fence, there will be ongoing electricity and maintenance costs.
- Please note that a properly anchored fence with a coyote roller on top along the whole perimeter of the yard is probably the best protective fencing you can have for your pets.

- To prevent coyotes from digging under chicken coops and similar places, and to add life to the barrier, spray on two coats of rustproof paint before installation. Always check for utility lines before digging in an area.
- Lay large flat stones, concrete patio pavers, or one-quarter-inch hardware cloth (held in place with stakes) on the surface of the soil next to the wall. The barrier forces coyotes to begin digging farther out, and they will most likely give up during the process.

R10. *An important message for parents and grandparents*

We cannot emphasize enough the importance of teaching children and grandchildren what to do if they encounter a coyote or an unfamiliar dog. Please take a few minutes to share this with your children and grandchildren:

- Never approach a coyote or dog you do not know.
- Never hold out your hand to a coyote or dog.
- Never feed a coyote or dog.
- If you see a coyote or dog, back away slowly from the animal, looking it directly in the eyes the entire time you are backing away until you can no longer see it.
- Never run from a coyote or dog.
- Scream, yell, wave your hands above your head, and make lots of loud noise, because wild animals do not like loud noises, and this will also let others know that you are in trouble.
- If you are near a hose, turn the hose on and squirt the coyote or dog.
- If rocks or similar objects are nearby, start throwing them in the direction of the coyote or dog, but not directly at it.

NOTES

1. Reynolds, R. (2012, August 14). Coyotes still rule; the Mile Square Park coyotes are still winning and feeding on our family pets. *Fountain Valley Patch.*

2. Burris, A. (2008, December 4). Coyotes kill pets, scare mobile home park residents. *The Orange County Register.*

3. Trout, J. (2001). *Solving coyote problems* (174). Lanham, MD: Lyons Press.

4. Baker, R. O. (2007). Wildlife Damage Management Conferences—Proceedings (58): *A review of successful urban coyote management programs implemented to prevent or reduce attacks on humans and pets in Southern California* (358). Lincoln, NE: University of Nebraska.

5. Caine, P. (Host). (2015, March 26). Chicago's urban coyotes (Television series episode—interview with Dr. Stanley Gehrt). *Chicago Tonight.* Chicago, IL: WTTW Chicago News.

6. Kim, A. (2012, October 7). Coyotes trouble Fountain Valley neighborhoods. *The Orange County Register.*

7. Trout, J. (2001). *Solving coyote problems* (133). Lanham, MD: Lyons Press.

8. Klein, A. (2013, July 22). 2-year-old recovering from coyote attack at Cypress cemetery. *The Orange County Register.*

9. News article. (2013, November 15). Emeil Hawkins, 3-year-old Chicago boy attacked by coyote after mistaking it for a dog. *The Huffington Post*.

10. Urban Coyote Research, Urban Coyote Ecology and Management. *Coyote relationships with other wildlife species*. Retrieved from http://www.urbancoyoteresearch.com/coyote-relationships-other-wildlife-species. Cook County, IL.

11. Mississippi State University Carnivore Ecology Research Project (1993). *Coyote (Canis latrans) influence of weather on movement and activity*. Retrieved from http://www.fwrc.msstate.edu/predator/coyInfluence.asp.

12. Valenzuela, B. (2014, June 1). Uptick in coyote sightings in Belmont Shore area. *Press Telegram*.

13. Mather, K. (2011, August 11). Seven coyotes killed after attacks on dogs in Laguna Woods. *Los Angeles Times*.

14. *Newscast. (2014, May 19). Coyote gets stuck on Huntington Beach wall (Television broadcast)*. Los Angeles, CA: KABC News.

15. Sahagan, L. (2014, December 17). In war on coyotes, some argue for learning to live with them. *Los Angeles Times*.

16. Tchekmedyian, A. (2014, August 1). Burbank man recalls being chased by a pack of coyotes. *Los Angeles Times*.

17. Karmarkar, J. (2014, August 27). Coyote snatches indoor cat in Laguna Woods. *The Orange County Register.*

18. Moreno, J. A., Yost, C., McDade, M. B., & Burch, W. (2014, September 22). Seal Beach council authorizes trapping, killing coyotes; residents pay tribute to dead pets (Television broadcast). Los Angeles, CA: KTLA 5 News.

19. Newscast. (2014, October 5). Demonstrators protest against coyote killings in Seal Beach (Television broadcast). Los Angeles, CA. CBS Los Angeles.

20. Orange County Public Works, OCGov.com. Retrieved from http://ocpublicworks.com/howdoi/view/santa_ana_river_projects.

21. Serna, J. (2014, October 14). Seal Beach will continue to trap, kill coyotes despite protests. *Los Angeles Times.*

22. Newscast. (2014, December 29). "I had to be there to save my son": Father describes fighting off coyote that bit 5-year-old boy (Television broadcast). San Francisco, CA: NBC Bay Area.

23. Mester, M. (2015, January 14). Ladera Ranch mom says coyote lunged at 10-month-old child, killed 2 dogs (Television broadcast). Los Angeles, CA: KTLA 5 News.

24. Frillman, C. (2015, February 24). The new war on rats. *Chicago Magazine.*

25. Caine, P. (Host). (2015, March 26). Chicago's urban coyotes (Television series episode—interview with Dr. Stanley Gehrt). *Chicago Tonight.* Chicago, IL: WTTW Chicago News.

26. Murphy, D. (2015, March 30). Coyote spends afternoon hanging out on roof of L.I.C. Bar in Queens. *New York Daily News.*

27. Baker, M. (Host). (2015, April 21). Multiple dens of coyotes spotted in Bergen County community (Television broadcast). New York, NY: CBS New York.

28. Velez, N. & O'Neill, N. (2015, May 7). Coyote spotted near LaGuardia Airport. *New York Post.*

29. Trout, J. (2001). *Solving coyote problems* (35). Lanham, MD: Lyons Press.

30. Tesky, J. L. (1995; revised 2013, July 18). Index of species information wildlife species: *Canis latrans.* Washington, D.C.: US Department of Agriculture, Forest Service, Rocky Mountain Research Station, Fire Sciences Laboratory. http://www.fs.fed.us/database/feis/.

31.   Trinh, J. (2015, September 30). Coyote bites 3-year-old girl in the neck at park playground. *LAIST.*

32.   Casiano, L., Jr. (2015, October 15). Man and 3-year-old son bitten by coyote in Irvine. *The Orange County Register.*

33.   Mojadad, I. (2015, November 4). Coyote responsible for three Irvine attacks euthanized, police said. *The Orange County Register.*

34.   Senk, A. (2015, November 5). Coyote sightings, attacks raise residents' hackles. *The Orange County Register.*

35.   MacBride, M. (Host). (2015, November 29). Coyote snatches Chihuahua from inside Laguna Beach home (Television broadcast). Los Angeles, CA: Eyewitness News ABC 7.

36.   Newscast. (2015, December 1). Coyote jumps through window at downtown Dallas Greyhound bus terminal (Television broadcast). Dallas, TX: WFAA News.

37.   Ramirez, K. (2016, April 15). Coyotes suspected following discovery of skeletal remains. *The Beachcomber,* XXIV(8).

INDEX

CHASING COYOTES

Composed in VTC SWITCHBLADE ROMANCE,
Lapture Display, and Palatino

www.ingramcontent.com/pod-product-compliance
Lightning Source LLC
Chambersburg PA
CBHW031152020426

42333CB00013B/623